THE NORTHERN TRAWL

The Story of Deep Sea Fishermen told in their own words

by Rupert Creed and Jim Hawkins
Music by John Connolly and Bill Meek

HUTTON PRESS
1986

Published by the Hutton Press Ltd.
130 Canada Drive, Cherry Burton, Beverley
North Humberside HU17 7SB

Text: Rupert Creed and Jim Hawkins

Songs: *The Northern Trawl; Trawling Trade; Trawlerman's Shanty; Another Morning; Lumpers Life; Harry Eddom; Pete's Tune; The Bionic Fisherman* – Copyright Maypole Music Ltd., London

Fiddler's Green – Copyright March Music, Chesterfield

Cover design: James Deighton, Hull

Photographs: Copyright Remould Theatre Co. and Grimsby Evening Telegraph

Printed by Clifford Ward & Co.
(Bridlington) Ltd.
55 West Street, Bridlington, East Yorkshire
YO15 3DZ

ISBN 0 907033 44 X

"The Northern Trawl"
is dedicated to all trawlermen who sailed from
Hull and Grimsby, and their families

ACKNOWLEDGEMENTS

The words of "The Northern Trawl" have been taken entirely from documentary archive material and tape-recorded interviews with the following, for the most part ex-trawlermen and their families:

John Carlill; Tony Scannell; Peter Grayburn; Brian Hodgson; George Rimmer; Stan Platten; Fred Blackburn; Olga Knight; Alice Harrison; Jack Butterick; Joseph Jenkinson; Ted Hales; Bill Hastie; Arthur Johnson; Frank and Betty Gladding; William Clarke; Frank Pepper; John and Alice Scarah; Jim Fuller; Mr. K. Doig; Mrs. V. Howard; Phil Johnson; Dot Pearson; Joseph Lowry; Ray Forsberg; John Glanville; Ron Bateman; Kevin MacNamara; Tom Boyd snr; Herbert and Katie Spencer; Harry Bolder; Yvonne Hartley; Linda Cox; Ken Cutsforth; Pat Hartley.

Further research material was provided by the following individuals and organisations:

Chris Russell, TGWU; Brenda Shaw; Phil Johnson; Dollie Hardie; the Town Docks Museum, Hull; the staff of the local history libraries in Hull and Grimsby; Ron Gibbins; the British Fishermen's Association.

The following people gave invaluable assistance in recording and typing the research material:

Thurstan Binns; Ruth Curtis; Debbie Clarke; Michelle Hesketh; Simon Beer; Mrs. Gwen Mackay; Anne Rhodes; Gwen Hudson; Mrs. F. Bancroft; Mrs. Slee-Lamb; Mrs. Lomax.

The tape and tape-recorders used in the interviews for "The Northern Trawl" were provided by BBC Radio Humberside, and training was given by Graham Henderson.

Boyd Line and J. Marr & Son made the trawlers "Arctic Corsair" and "Jacinta" available to the Remould Theatre Company for research, training and publicity.

The publishers wish to thank the following for their generous co-operation and assistance in the production of the book:

James Deighton for permission to reproduce his design on the front cover.
Averil Coult, Administrator of the Remould Theatre Company.
Maypole Music Ltd., London, and March Music, Chesterfield, for permission to reproduce the lyrics of the songs by John Conolly and Bill Meek; also John Conolly for his help in obtaining this permission.
Dave Whatt for the cast production photographs and rear cover photograph.

The staff of the Grimsby Evening Telegraph, in particular George Black, for making available the series of photographs taken aboard the "Arsenal."
Stan Platten of Hull for his assistance in compiling captions for these photographs.

REMOULD THEATRE COMPANY

CAST LIST AND PRODUCTION STAFF

"The Northern Trawl" was first performed by The Remould Theatre Company on September 30th, 1985, at Howden Junior School, Humberside, with the following cast:

JIM — Iain Macrae
STAN — Chuck Foley
MAUREEN — Ingrid Wells
TED — Buster Scott
RON — Andrew Watson

On subsequent tours the part of Ron was played by Philip Green

The set was designed by Dave Whatt

The music was composed by John Conolly and Bill Meek

Administration, publicity and costume design by Averil Coult

Stage Management — Richard J. Kennaugh
Charles Millward

Musical Directors — Hilary Gordon and Jim Hawkins

Production and
Administrative Assistants — Ruth Curtis and Sara Hawkins

Technical Advisors — Stan Platten and John Carlill

Publicity Design — James Deighton

The play was directed by Rupert Creed

The stage production of "The Northern Trawl" was commissioned and funded by Humberside County Council Leisure Services and Lincolnshire & Humberside Arts, with financial assistance from Hull City Council. Subsequent national touring was funded by the Arts Council of Great Britain.

INTRODUCTION

"The Northern Trawl" is a play with music that tells the story of the deep sea trawlermen who sailed from Hull and Grimsby to fish the hostile Arctic waters off Greenland, Iceland and Russia. It is a story of hardship, humour, courage and tragedy. It is the story of an industry that has now virtually disappeared, of a once thriving community robbed of its traditional livelihood. It is a story ultimately of betrayal and bitterness.

But "The Northern Trawl" is not simply a play *about* fishermen — it has actually been *written by* fishermen. Although the two writers Rupert Creed and Jim Hawkins are responsible for the selection of material and the structuring of the final play, the words themselves and the incidents portrayed have not been invented by the writers, but have been taken direct from hours of tape recorded interviews with ex-trawlermen and their families from Hull and Grimsby. All the incidents portrayed in the play actually happened in real life, and are here described by the fishermen that were witness to the events: "The Northern Trawl" is their story, told in their own words.

Preparatory work on the project started in 1984. The Remould Theatre Comnpany had been based in Hull since its formation in 1981, and the company's work had always aimed at reaching as wide an audience in Humberside and Lincolnshire as possible. To this end we had written and produced plays for children and adults, performed events for local community groups, and toured to theatres, community centres and village halls in all parts of the region. We increasingly felt however that the company's work could be extended further into the community and thus "The Northern Trawl" was born with two main objectives: to produce a play whose subject matter was relevant to the area, and to actively involve the local community in the creation of the play.

With funding from Humberside Leisure Services and Lincolnshire & Humberside Arts, work on the project started in May 1985. We advertised in the press and on local radio for people who had worked in the fishing industry, in whatever capacity, to contact us so that we could record their stories and reminiscences. We set up a team of volunteers to assist in the interviews and help with the mammoth task of typing up transcripts of each recording. We liaised with BBC Radio Humberside who publicised the project and offered us tape and the use of Uher tape recorders which enabled us to make recordings of a professional standard, which in turn could be broadcast in a series of programmes about the fishing industry. After a training session at Radio Humberside we were ready to embark on the recordings.

The response from the trawlermen was overwhelming and over a period of three months we recorded the stories and reminiscences of over 40 people who had worked in the industry, resulting in approximately 50 hours of tape recorded material plus a mountain of press cuttings, photographs and personal memoirs. Most of the recordings were done in Hull but we also spent several days in Grimsby, as well as making trips to small towns and villages throughout the region. The recordings were made mainly in people's homes, but we also had some useful sessions in the pubs down Hessle Road in Hull, which was the centre of the now defunct fishing industry.

During this period John Conolly and Bill Meek from Grimsby were commissioned to write the music for the play. Well known on the folk scene, John and Bill were the driving force behind the folk band 'Broadside' and more recently 'Rational Anthem.' Many of the songs they had already written about the fishing industry, such as 'Trawling Trade' and 'Fiddler's Green,' were ideal as they were, but the title song, 'Pete's Tune' and 'Bionic Fisherman' were composed specially for the production.

In August 1985, Jim Hawkins and myself started putting the script together from the transcripts of the tape recordings. We set ourselves a ground rule that the play should not simply be a sequence of stories that are told, but that are relived in the telling. We also avoided a purely documentary approach, so dates, facts and figures tend to be omitted in preference to presenting a picture of the industry as seen through the eyes of the men who lived through it all. The result is a play with a deliberately fluid action — the actors take on characters as required, shifting from straight narrative sections to enacted scenes, and mixing the two when necessary.

The cast was assembled and the play rehearsed in September, and great care was taken to ensure that the actors fully understood and assimilated the work and lifestyle of actual fishermen. We spent time on a trawler in dock with two ex-trawlermen who acted as technical advisors on the production. They explained to the cast the work and the machinery on board a trawler and also sat in on rehearsals to advise and correct where necessary.

"The Northern Trawl" opened in October 1985 and the success of the first tour ensured subsequent tours in the Spring and Autumn of 1986. The emotional impact of the play went beyond what we expected. With an audience of trawlermen and their families there was a constant commentary of approval and confirmation that we had got their story right, but the play was equally effective with an audience of 'outsiders.' Many places we toured to had no connection with fishing at all and yet the enthusiastic response proved that the play was an effective piece of theatre in its own right. Mining is a comparable industry to fishing in terms of the danger, hardship and the sense of community that the job instills, but unlike mining, the fishing industry has never received much exposure on television, film or stage, and I think that audiences were genuinely amazed at the insight into the job that the play offered.

"The Northern Trawl" is a play with many authors — it is the distillation of countless people's experience and knowledge accumulated over a lifetime's work in the fishing industry. Whether you are reading this with a view to performance, or to learn something about a vanished way of life, or simply to relive a few memories of your own, I hope that the play will give you as much pleasure in the reading as it did in the making.

Rupert Creed
May, 1986

THE NORTHERN TRAWL

There are no set characters as such in this play, but for convenience sake each of the five roles has been given a name:

RON — A young lad, enthusiastic and green. Ron plays the deckie-learner roles.
TED — Middle-aged trawlerman. Ted takes the skipper's roles. In the original production he also played keyboards which were located on the bridge.
JIM — A Scots deckhand.
STAN — A Hull deckhand
MAUREEN — A Hull fisherman's wife.

The five actors also sing and play all the music in the play.

In the original production, the split level set, designed by Dave Whatt, was used to suggest the various locations of above and below decks and the bridge of a trawler, quayside and pub bar.

ACT ONE

THE NORTHERN TRAWL

Jim: *(Solo)*
We're the hundred year haulers, we're trawling again
We'll show you disaster, our laughter and pain
We'll show you the fishing and stand proud once more
The sea flows in our blood, so be damned to the shore
And whatever fates send, we'll live to the end
A life on the northern trawl.

All:
We're the hundred year haulers and we've seen it all
A century of history from this dockyard wall
Seen the whalers decline and the Brixham men come
Seen the hopeful sail out and the lucky sail home
And down all the days we've passed on the ways
Of life on the northern trawl.

We've watched the sails furled and the steam age take o'er
We've watched the steel rail spread to harbour and shore
Seen the owners grow fat on the profits they made
Heard the price that was bid, seen the price that was paid
And through all the years we've lived with the fears
Of life on the northern trawl.

North to Norway and Faroe we've followed the shoals
We found the White Sea where the ice ocean rolls
Took our fleets and our men to the Arctic's far shores
Then lost them again in the war to end wars
And though many died we still talk with pride
Of life on the northern trawl.

We're the hundred year haulers, we're trawling again
We'll show you disaster, our laughter and pain
We'll show you the fishing and stand proud once more
The sea flows in our blood so be damned to the shore
And whatever fates send we'll live till the end
A life on the northern trawl.

Jim: *(Solo.)* And whatever fates send, we'll live till the end

All: A life on the northern trawl.

SCENE ONE

Stan: St. Andrews Dock, 'Ull. Home of the British deep sea fishing industry.

Ron: It were built in 1883.

Jim: Extended 1897.

Ted: It's got nineteen and a half acres of water space.

Maureen: And six 'undred and twelve thousand, three 'undred and seventy square feet of covered markets.

Stan: Set foot in St. Andrews Dock and you was in another world.

They break to various positions. Ron is a barrow lad pushing a bobber's trolley. Jim is a bobber on the first level. Stan is a bobber on the stage. They mime the work of swinger and weighman. Ted is on stage level checking off imaginary kits of fish. Maureen is on the first level miming doing her face waiting for her husband to dock.

Stan: Coal for yer 'ole.

Jim: Coal for yer 'ole.

Stan: Coal for money.

Jim: Coal for money.

Stan: Red Army.

Jim: Red Army.

Ron: There was forever a movement because you have t' imagine, twenty or thirty ships a day coming and going.

Maureen: It was a shuttle service shifting in and out the dock at every tide.

Ted: There was the fishermen who caught the fish. . .

Ron: And next on at two in the morning, were the bobbers to unload it.

Stan: Owd sowdiers.

Jim: Owd sowdiers.

Ted: And after the bobbers had gone home, that's when the ancillary workers moved in.

Stan: There was coal 'eaving, purring coal on ship.

Maureen: 'Cos they was all steam ships, they was all coal burners in them days.

Ron: There was cleaning boilers out, what you call boiler scaling.

Stan: And gangs o' men descended on ships with 'ammers and scrapers.

Jim: And we literally had to handchip, to remove all the paint off the ship.

Ted: There was rope works, Gorricks, Coal Salt and Tan.

Ron: There was rully men, coal wagons, coal trains. . .

Maureen: And then there was the fish houses where they made the fish manure.

All: Pooh.

Ron: And that was an atrocious smell.

Stan: But the fish that was landed, that was fresh fish. It 'ad an earthy smell, a natural smell.

Jim: There was North Sea Market, Iceland Market. . .

Ron: There was five, six, seven, as high as eight or nine ships laid alongside.

Maureen: And on nice days, all the mothers, wives and girlfriends would go down the dock to see their husbands or fathers in.

They break. Stan is wheeled round on the trolley by Ron as if the ship was docking. Jim is a bum on the quayside. Maureen is waiting for her husband. Ted goes up to the bridge.

Stan: 'Lo Jim.

Jim: Hello Stan.

Maureen: Hello luv.

Ted: There was money passed over to them that was out of a ship.

Ron: What you call back 'anders.

Stan: How long have you been 'ome?

Jim: Oh, about a fortnight.

Stan: Are you skint?

Jim: Yeh.

Stan: *(Throws a packet of fags to him.)* See yer in Rayners.

Stan, Ron and Ted mime drinking.

Maureen: It was always the same. First night 'ome they'd be in the boozer with their mates. Crawled 'ome, never come 'ome sober. The neighbours'd be shouting, 'Hey Moo, there's your Stan coming.' 'Where?' And they'd say 'There, 'ave a look.' And there he was, crawling along on all fours. Like a dog he was, paralytic.

Ron and Stan mime throwing up.

Ted: Aye, it's true what she says. I'd say that seventy percent of the fishermen was the same — we'd all have too much to drink the first night home.

Stan: But next day we'd go out together, do a bit of shopping...

Maureen: New coat, new 'andbag...

Ron: Buy summat for lads...

Maureen: Trip to the Tivoli, big slapup meal...

Ted: It was the same routine, trip after trip.

Stan: And before you knew it, you was back off to sea again.

Ron and Stan break, miming pulling a piano along on the trolley.

Jim: And there was one time the crew of the St. Matthew bought an old piano down the Hessle Road. And they brought it down to the dock on a hand cart and they got the crane driver to lift it onto the ship.

Maureen: And then the manager comes out.

Ted: *(As Manager.)* Eh! You're not sailing with that piano. Put it back on the dock.

Maureen: And back it goes on the dock.

With Jim miming the crane.

And then the crew says...

Ron/Stan: Oi, put it back on the ship.

Maureen: And back it goes on the ship.

Ted: On the dock.

Ron/Stan: On the ship.

Ted: Dock.

Ron/Stan: Ship.

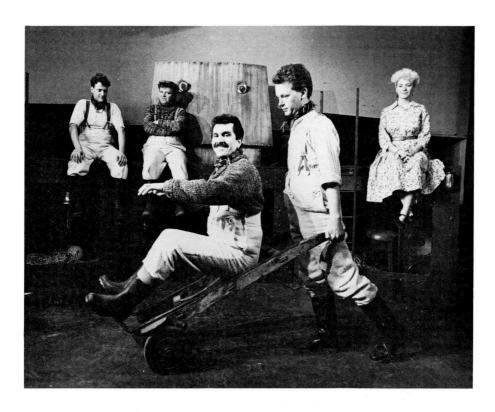

Act 1 Scene 1. Piano on ship story.

Ted: Dock.

Ron/Stan: Ship.

Etc...

Jim: Bloody 'ell.

Maureen: So in the end the crew says...

Stan: You either purr it back on the ship or we don't sail.

Maureen: And back it goes on the ship and out they go through the lock gates with one of 'em playing the piano.

Ron wheels Stan off with Stan miming a quick burst of melody played for real by Ted. Jim jumps down to stage level and is then joined by Ron and Stan.

Jim: Aye, St. Andrew's Dock. There was a million jobs just crying out for men.

Stan: If you got fed up with one, you chucked it and went somewhere else.

Ron: At that time, if someone 'd said fishing 'd disappear out of 'Ull, they'd 'ave been taken to nut factory.

Ted and Maureen play 'Pete's Tune' over:

Stan: We knew when we was kids that fishing was gonna be our job. We never said. . .

Ron: I'm gonna be a train driver.

Jim: I'm gonna drive an aeroplane.

Stan: We never said we was gonna be fishermen, but somehow we all knew what we was gonna do.

Ron: And we knew all about fishing 'cos of our 'olidays. We didn't 'ave 'olidays like normal people. Our 'oliday was three weeks in summer down Arctic fishing ground. Our teaching period.

Stan: Pleasuring we called it.

Jim: We knew all the dock signals, we knew all the ships. . .

Ron: You could look out from St. Andrews Dock where the 'Umber bends round to Grimsby, the 'elbow' we called it, and you could tell exactly what ship just by its outline.

Stan: You was educated to the job before you left school.

Ron: And you saw ships going away and you 'eard tales of men making fabulous amounts o' money, and the next step for a lad of fourteen was to go to sea as a deckie learner.

Music stops.

Stan: 'Ere. Our kid 'ere wants to go to sea. You'd berrer sign 'im on.

Jim: You're sixteen aren't yer?

Ron: Aye. Course I'm sixteen.

Jim: Sign 'ere then.

Stan: And with that he was on.

SCENE TWO

They break. Stan and Jim go to the bunks stage centre. Maureen becomes a night watchman on the first level. Ron is also on the first level.

Ron: I was ordered for four in the morning, but being keen like I got there two hours early. And I went on deck to look for a walk-in focsle but I couldn't find it so I went aft to watchman. Can you tell us where focsle is?

Maureen: It's forrard.

Ron: Aye, but I've been forrard and I can't find it.

Maureen: Right bloody Christmas cracker 'ere. Come on, I'll show yer.

14

Ron: So we goes forrard to iron foundry where they keep all the chains and shackles. And he opens this big door, then he lifts up this hatch. It's a wooden 'atch, about two foot square. What, down there?

Maureen: Aye, be careful, it's a straight ladder.

Ron: So I drops me kitbag down and it sounded like a bloody week before it hit the bottom.

Stan: You always slept forrard in the old ships.

Jim: Mulberry Flats we called 'em.

Stan: Two rows of bunks, two or three 'igh.

Rob: But in this ship they were seven high. They went right from deck level down to keel, that's how deep they were.

Stan: In the middle was a big pipe for the anchor chain.

Jim: And a coal stove. A big round Bogy stove.

Ron: And I thought 'Bloody 'ell. What have I let meself in for 'ere?'

Ted: *(Entering below.)* You always tried to get on board first and get yer gear in a bottom bunk.

Jim: And there were arguments.

Stan: I was 'ere last trip. This is my bunk.

Ted goes up to higher bunk.

Jim: And you had to provide yer own bedding. What we called a 'donkey's breakfast.'

Ted: It was an old straw mattress.

Stan: And they was bad. You 'ad bugs, cockroaches, fleas. And you got thrown all over the place. But nobody seemed to bother.

Ron: *(Now on stage level.)* The thing is, they 'ad atmosphere. There was summat about 'em where everybody was 'appy. When you got the lights on and the stove going, and everybody spinning a yarn, it was a real good atmosphere.

Jim: *(Handing Ron drink.)* There y'are, snacker. Get that down yer.

Ron: Oh, ta.

Ted: Eh, did you 'ear about old Clarky, you know, the Grimsby lad?

Jim: Wharr about 'im?

Ted: 'E got done for being drunk last week. He comes up before the magistrate, old Smithhurst, and Smithhurst says, 'Ten shillings or seven days.' And Clarky says, 'Oh I'll have the ten shillings please.'

Stan: Bloody Yellerbelly.

15

Jim: There was this Grimmy I knew, and he gets paid off like, and he thinks to 'imself, 'I'm going to get me own back on that gaffer.' And the gaffer's got this chicken farm you see, so he goes down to the chicken farm, breaks in, and steals all the birds. But he leaves a message behind and it says 'Robbed the rich to feed the poor, left cock and hen to breed some more.'

Stan: Eh snacker, how many fingers 'ave we got between us?

Ron: Well, thirty.

All: No.

Ron: Twenty eight?

All: No.

Ron: Twenty six?

All: No.

Ron: And then they all 'eld their 'ands out to show me 'ow many they 'ad.

Jim: Twenty five, and a half.

Ron: 'Cos like they'd all lost fingers in accidents with wires and winches and warps.

Jim: One guy I knew, he got frostbite that bad, that he had to lie in his bunk with his hand in a bucket of water. And they wouldn't let him see a doctor or anything. And his fingers went rotten, pure green they were. You could smell 'em way down in the mess deck.

Ted: I knew this bloke from Scarborough. He always used to go third hand. She took a heavy sea one day and washed him off the winch aft. So he picked himself up after the ship had cleared herself of water and he found out his right arm had been pulled out the socket. Well he looks over to the casing side, and there's his arm stuck in the stop sheave. And he didn't even know 'e'd done it.

Stan: My brother-in-law got smashed up one trip. I was learning 'im the job and you've got this preventer, a chain what you put over the warps. Anyhow, instead of 'im waiting, he puts the chain on before the warps'd been properly blocked up. And as luck would 'ave it, the 'ook parted. 'An it 'it this brother-o-law o' mine, went straight through 'is new oilfrock, and knocked 'im on the kedge anchor. He got all 'is face bashed in, his face was like a football when I picked 'im up. I just flaked out. I was in a right state. And do you know what the skipper said? 'E said, ''E only did that to get off the deck.'

Ron: What's the old man like 'ere then?

Ted: Ooh, you've got to watch yer baccy, haven't yer Stan?

Stan: Aye, keep yer baccy locked up.

Ron: How do yer mean?

Jim: The last time we were hauling, we were getting all the gear in, and there's

16

nothing but a great big heap of mud. And the skipper's there and he's laughing away, 'It'll take you a bit to shift that, boys, it'll take you a bit to shift that.'

Ted: And you wanted to use the donkey, didn't you?

Jim: Aye, but he says 'Oh no, I don't want no donkey on that, I want every sole out of that mud if there is any.'

Stan: And about an hour or so after that I says to Jock, 'You go down the berth quiet like and have a look round,' 'cos I 'ad an idea, see.

Jim: So I goes down and there's the skipper and he's got all the crew's baccy tins laid out on the table, all the lads' baccy tins, and he's pinching a wee bit out of every tin. So I says to him, 'Eh, what you doing with that baccy?' And he says 'What you doing off that deck?' So I says to him, not in a very nice way I might say, 'You, get that baccy back in them tins now.' And I goes back on the deck.

Stan: Aye, then we both went down.

Jim: He's got him by the scruff of his neck. . .

Stan: I was that bloody angry.

Jim: We're holding him out over the rail. . .

Stan: Any more of that on this trip and that's you in the drink.

Jim: We're going to let you go skipper, we're going to let you go.

Stan: He ain't said owt since has he?

Jim: No.

Ted: He's noted for it though, pinching the lads' baccy. Too bloody mean to buy it himself.

Stan: But don't you try owt like that, snacker, you'll get yourself bloody shot.

Jim: You just do as yer told and keep out of the road of the boys working.

Ted: And remember, the skipper, 'e's god, and the mate, 'e's undergod.

Ron: And me, I was under the ship's cat as far as seniority went but I sat there and I took it all in and I thought, 'Yeh, this is the life for me.'

Jim: And you learnt about the pierhead jump that trip didn't you, snacker?

Ron: Oh aye.

Stan: Now yer pierhead jump, that's peculiar to the fishing industry. What happens is, your ship's in dock ready to sail and one of the crew ain't turned up.

Ted: He's drunk.

Jim: Or in bed with somebody.

Stan: Or whatever. But yer tide's running up fast, you've got a good 'ead o' steam, and yer skipper's on the bridge mouthing profanities. . .

17

Jim: And all the crew's leaning out over the rail waiting for the last minute taxi...

Ted: No taxi.

Stan: But among yer dockside bums you'd perhaps somebody who knows a bit about trawling...

Ted: Or not.

Stan: And at the very last minute he literally jumps onto the ship off the quay, the ropes are cast off, and away he goes to sea for a trip. And that's yer pierhead jump. You've done it yerself ain't yer, Ted?

Ted: Oh aye.

Jim: Aye, and it got you into a bit of trouble with missus, didn't it?

Maureen: You're bloody right it did. He went away for three weeks and I didn't even know 'e'd gone. Just disappeared.

Ted: You see the theory of pierhead jumps is...

Maureen: Shut up, I'm telling it. The theory is somebody on the dockside is supposed to come and tell the dear wife that her husband's gorr a ship. Only nobody did. I didn't know where 'e'd got to. I thought 'e'd done a bunkoff and I've got three kids like. Anyhow 'e turns up three weeks later in the same clothes 'e went away in.

Ted: Well, I'd just slipped out for a quick pint.

Maureen: What 'ad 'appened was nobody on board ship 'ad any gear to lend 'im, so for three weeks, 'e'd slept and gutted in the same clothes 'e left 'Ull in. And 'e stank o' fish. Anyow, 'e's standing at the door with 'is money in 'is 'and...

Ted: Well, I daren't go straight to the boozer.

Maureen: I takes one look at 'im and I punches 'im straight on the nose, blood everywhere.

Ted: She didn't give us time to explain anything.

Maureen: I cuts all 'is clothes off and bungs 'em on the kitchen fire, and then 'e says to me 'Are we going out tonight?' So I says 'You're not going nowhere.' 'Why not?' ''Cos I've pawned your other bloody suit.'

Blackout.
The actors regroup.

SCENE THREE

Ron: That first trip, I'll never forget it. I was sick, I mean continuously sick for three weeks. And they kept stuffing bread down me.

Stan: Well, to bring stuff up you've got to put stuff down.

Ron: I was teased, 'ad me leg pulled.

Jim: Gerrus a left handed spanner kid.

Ted: It's only a gentle breeze that, snacker.

Ron: And it was blowing an 'urricane. I didn't know whether me stomach was in me mouth or what was 'appening. I was cold, I was tired, and I wanted me mother. And me arms felt they belonged to Morgan the Mighty, and every time I bent down I thought me back'd break.

Ted: It was the same for all of us. You got used to it.

Stan: After a few trips your 'ands was nearly double the size with the 'ard skin and calluses. You could stick a pin in anywhere in yer 'and and you wouldn't even feel it.

Stan and Ron break to new positions. Stan is mending nets. Ron is standing cold and miserable.

Jim: The first time I went to sea, we were in this ship off Bear Island. My dad was there at the time. He was bosun that trip.

Maureen: I was dead against it. 'I'm taking the lad to sea,' 'e said. 'Over my dead body,' I said. But they sneaked out the house, didn't they.

Jim: And it was blowing and freezing and I'd been up about forty hours and I was only a kid. And I stood against the needle basket and if anything happened to those needles, boy you had it.

Ron: Eh, Dad. Dad, I'm tired. Can I go and get a liedown?

Stan: You bloody stop there and look after yer job, or yer get yer bloody 'ead kicked in.

Jim: And me dad pulled on the codend and suddenly... *(Loud discord on keyboards.)* A corpse fell out of the trawl.

Stan: It's a bloke.

Jim: The smell was terrible. There was skin hanging off his face, there was flesh hanging down where fish had been feeding, there were prawns all over him. Then this guy says...

Ted: Eh, that's a good pair o' boots that. That's a good pair o' leather boots.

Jim: And he pulled and he pulled and the bloody leg came off. *(Ted falls over backward clutching imaginary leg.)* Well, that did it, I was sick as a pig. *(Ron throws up.)* But eventually they gets the boots off and heaves the body back over the side.

Ron: I 'eard stories like and I used to listen to 'em but I thought, is that part of the life? Am I going to end up like that? But then again, I daren't ask anybody.

Jim: But that night we decided we were going to play a trick on the bloke with the boots, so we got ourselves chains and bits and rattled them outside his bunk.

Stan and Maureen rattle chains above Ted, who is asleep in the bunk.

Stan: Whooooo...

Maureen: Where's me boots. I want me boots...

Ted: *(Waking up.)* Bloody 'ell. It's a piece o' toast...

Maureen: Where's me boots. I want me boots...

Ted: Oh, Christ...

Jim: So he grabs his boots and chucks them back over the side.

Ted: *(About to throw them into audience.)* Oh. Port side *(Throws them backstage.)* There's yer boots. Now leave me alone.

Jim: He was as white as a sheet.

Ron: And I was still being sick coming up the 'Umber, and I thought, I ain't going again.

Stan: But the thing was when you gorr 'ome with an 'andful o' fivers, you forgot about the bad times 'cos you was a millionaire for a day.

Ron: Aye, twelve quid I got on that trip, and for a lad of fourteen, twelve quid was a lot of money.

Ted: There's 'im walking down the dock with his chest stuck out.

Ron: I couldn't feel me legs to be honest. If there'd been a coal wagon alongside I'd 'ave knocked it into the dock with the sway I 'ad.

Maureen: He comes rushing into the 'ouse and gives me a fiver. You know, one of them old fashioned white ones. And I says to 'im, 'You're going back then?'

Pause.

Ron: Aye, course I'm going back.

TRAWLING TRADE

Stan:
North to the Faroe Islands, south to the coast of Spain
West with the whaling fleet and off to the Pole again
Over the world of water, seventeen seas I've strayed
Now to the north I'm sailing, back to the trawling trade.

All: *Chorus.*
Come ye bold seafaring men, there's fortunes to be made
In the trawling trade.

Stan:
Back to the midnight landings, back to the fishdock smell
Back to the frozen wind as hard as the teeth of hell
Back to the strangest game that ever a man has played
Follow the stormy rollers back to the trawling trade.

All: *Chorus.*

Stan:
Down with yer trawling tackle, down with yer nets and gear
Wait for the winches winding, wait for the deckies cheer
Up with the shining harvest glittering silver sprayed
Down to the decks below to pay for the trawling trade.

All: *Chorus.*

Instrumental verse and chorus.

All:
Home with a harvest wind and back to the Humber tide
Run to the starboard rail and leap to the water's side
Roll with a roaring bunch of fishermen newly paid
Down to the dockside pubs and drink to the trawling trade.

Chorus and end.

SCENE FOUR

The actors regroup.

Jim: We were employed on a casual basis from trip to trip, so you never knew if you might get the sack.

Stan: You could be the finest worker in the world but if the skipper din't like yer face, if the mate din't like yer face, you were out.

Ron: Spragged.

Jim: Walkabout.

Maureen: And when their spragging time was up, six months, possibly longer, they'd probably get their job back, but they 'ad to learn to keep their mouth shut.

Ted: I was mate on a ship and we was having trouble with the middle fish room, all the fish was going bad, so I said to the boss, 'There's only one thing I can suggest sir, and that's a new middle fish room.' And he says. . .

Jim: It's cheaper to get a new mate — sack.

Ted: Just like that.

Ron: Another time this ship came in late and all the fish had gone off so the gaffer comes down the dock to have a look at it.

They regroup with Stan as the gaffer. Others stand waiting for the inevitable response.

All: Morning sir, etc. . . . .

Stan: *(Inspecting imaginary kits of fish.)* Shit. Pile of bloody shit. Who's the mate?

Ted: Quinn sir.

Stan: You'd better take a rest for a trip or two, Quinn. *(Goes to leave.).*

Jim: *(As Quinn.)* Oi. If it's shit we've landed I think you'd better have a closer look.

Jim lifts up Stan and turns him upside down.

Ted: And he picks him up, turns him upside down and shoves him headfirst into the kit of fish.

Ron: But he never got another ship out of 'Ull.

Maureen: And they blacked 'im in Grimsby.

Ted: He 'ad to bloody emigrate to get a job.

Jim releases Stan.

Jim: And that's the powers that they had. They could even take you to court for missing a ship.

Ted: And if you didn't pay yer fine, off you went to jail. *(Goes up to bridge.).*

Maureen: It's laughable. It's like missing a train and going to jail for it.

Ron: There's no other job in the world where you get fined for not working.

Stan: And that's how they did it. That's how they kept us under their thumbs. You were their serfs, you were their deckhands.

Jim: They owned the fish houses, the curing house, the ice house, you name it, they even owned the stores where you got yer gear.

Ron: Yer frocks, boots, mittens, knives. . .

Jim: And all this was stopped off yer settling sheet when you got home, and it wasn't like you could go some place else for yer gear, 'cos they had the monopoly.

Ted: I tell ya, if Al Capone had known what went on in those days, he'd have turned in his grave with what he missed out on.

Maureen: But when they gorr a ship, it was like the sun was shining. They were full of the joys of spring, they were off to sea.

'Pete's Tune' starts. Maureen exits. Others regroup. Ron is 'on deck' peeling spuds. Stan is below deck as 'trimmer' miming shovelling coal. Jim is miming setting up the shelving in fish room. Ted is the skipper on the bridge. Music over Ted:

Ted: The skipper was more or less free to go where he wanted. Meself, I preferred White Sea or Bear Island. And in the summer you had the midnight sun, you had daylight all the time. And going through the fijords, the scenery was fantastic. It was so narrow in places you could almost touch the sides. And we'd see reindeer. Reindeer would cross in front of the ship, and the pilot'd slow the ship down to let them cross. And Spitsbergen, it was out of this world. I once fished so close to the shore, you could hear the water lapping up onto the beach. And above was this great beautiful iceberg mountain. It was fairyland, absolute fairyland. *(Music stops.)* Of course a lot of the lads didn't appreciate it. Some of them didn't even look at it.

Stan: I couldn't bloody look at it. I was down below trimming coal.

Ron: You see in the old coal burning ships, yer after fishroom was loaded full of coal and when you was steaming to yer fishing ground you 'ad to trim all this coal through a tunnel to the stokehold for the firemen to fire the ship.

Stan: It was 'ard work an' all, you was teaming in sweat.

Jim: And in the forrard fishroom you had to set up all yer shelves and staging ready for the fish. And at the fore end here you literally had a big wall of ice which you had to chop into little pieces and shovel into the pounds. Ice-cracking we called it.

Ron: You carried coal on deck too. I seen ships coming out of dock that loaded up, they've been half under the water, like a submarine.

Stan: And when you'd trimmed enough coal from the after fishroom you opened an 'atch on deck and shovelled it in.

Ted: And that could be dangerous. 'Cos with the ship so low in the water, it would just take one big sea and you could be swamped.

Jim: There were other dangers too. 'Cos you slept forrard you had to cross the open deck to get aft, and there's been many a man lost just changing watches on a night.

Ron: You 'ad to chance yer luck. You saw a sea, you waited. And you 'ad that feeling, you knew just when to go. Nine times out of ten you were right.

Ted: Decent skippers would ease the ship in and put her head to wind, that way you give the crew a chance to get across.

Stan: Aye, but some of the buggers wouldn't. Too keen to get to the fish.

Ron: One skipper I knew, he lost four men on one trip.

Jim: I knew a skipper who lost his own son off the deck. Never even batted an eyelid. Just carried on fishing right to the end of the trip.

Stan: And you 'adn't to be selective as regards yer living either.

Ron: Where's the shithouse?

Stan/Ron/Jim: He's on the bridge.

23

Ted: Oi.

Jim: The toilet facilities were really primitive in those days, so if it was bad weather you had to go down to the stokehold and do yer business on a shovel, and chuck it into the furnace. And if you didn't get rid of it properly, you copped hell off the engineer.

Stan: But in fine weather we'd do it off the rail. It's true, we'd hang off the side.

Ron: Flying a pigeon, we called it.

Stan and Jim mime the business.

Ted: Not very hygienic.

Stan: One bloke came down to do his stuff and I was trimmer at the time and I 'id in the bunkers. And instead of 'im doing it on a shovel he made a little pile of coal. *(Jim mimes all of this.)* When he turned round, I got me shovel and I put it under his backside.

Jim: Oooh.

Stan: And when he'd finished I brought it back into the bunkers. Well he turned round, he didn't know where to look. He thought he'd done it up the wall. And when he'd finished, I put it back, and then the engineer came down.

Jim: *(As if protesting to the engineer.)* I couldna find it. I couldna find it.

Stan: Did he get a rollicking.

Blackout. 'Pete's Tune.' Maureen enters. Ron, Stan and Jim exit. Music over.

SCENE FIVE

Maureen: I never used to worry about 'im in the summertime but when the winter came in, the fog and the snow and the ice, that was the time I worried.

Ted: Leaving home early morning tide. Midnight, one o' clock, that was the worst.

Maureen: I'd never see him to the door. Sometimes I didn't even get up.

Ted: It was just the one thought — will we ever see each other again.

Maureen: I 'ad to be mother and father to the kids.

Ted: I was a stranger to me own bairns. I hardly knew them.

Maureen: I 'ad to be strict with them at times. It was no use saying wait till yer father gets home.

Ted: I never smacked 'em while I was in dock, 'cos it played on me mind when I was at sea.

Maureen: I couldn't sleep on a night. I used to think about 'im out there on the water.

Ted: But that was the way of life. You were fishermen. You went to sea. That was the job.

Music stops.

Maureen: But I 'ave to admit it. I did enjoy me independence. When they was away you knew what you 'ad to do, and you could get on with it. And some of us were devils. I used to go out regular. Four or five of us wives would go out and we'd 'ave a really good time. You see there used to be a lot of these Danish sailors about — 'scrobs' we called 'em. And we'd go looking for these scrobs 'cos they 'ad all the money to spend on us. Oh and some of those Danish boys, they were beautiful. They were, they were beautiful men. Oh but it did cause trouble. You see there'd be fishermen out of work and they'd see us with these scrobs and they'd tell our husbands when they came back into dock. And our 'usbands 'd go round, they'd find 'em out and they'd play 'ell with 'em. There'd be a good old punch up in the street, fists flying, blood all over the place. And then they'd all go out and have a drink together. Yeah, I could never understand it. You 'ad a face like a butcher's shop and the bloke that's done it is yer mate and you go and have a pint together. But then, that's fishermen.

Maureen exits. Ron, Stan and Jim enter in full sea gear.

SCENE SIX

Ron/Stan/Jim: *(Singing.)* Come ye bold seafaring men, there's fortunes to be made, in the trawling trade.

Ted: When you got to the fishing grounds, that's when the work really started. You got all yer nets ready and prepared to shoot yer first trawl.

Stan: On the old sidewinders, you nearly always shot yer gear from the starboard side of the ship, so the skipper would stop his engines and lay the ship starboard side to the wind.

Jim: You had to do that 'cos if the wind was on the port side you'd end up with the ship over yer gear and get it all tackled up.

Ted: And shooting side to wind was in itself a hazard 'cos the ship would lay there helpless in the water and in bad weather the seas'd come rolling across that deck.

Ron: And you weren't covered up or owt, you were out in the open. Used to be hung over the side half the time.

Stan: The first thing you did was you got yer codend over.

Ron: Now yer codend is the end bit of the net where all yer fish end up. Like a toe of a sock.

All: Heave.

Stan: Then you got the rest of yer trawl out, the belly, the baitings and what have you.

Ron: And there could be two hundred foot o' net going over the side, and you'd better be careful you don't get yer feet in the way of that net, or over you go with it.

All: Heave.

Ted: And the ship'd pull away from the gear until it comes tight to yer set of bobbins about sixty odd foot in length.

Stan: And you get yer bobbins up over the top and everybody had to push to gerr 'em over the ship's side and into the water.

All: Heave. . . splash.

Ron: And you 'ad a couple of ground cables that run to yer Dan Lenos.

Jim: Yer Dan Lenos are two big metal balls that roll along the sea bed and help spread the wings of the trawl.

Stan: And these was fastened to yer fore and aft gallows which were two angled towers at the side of the ship.

Ron: And away go yer Dan Lenos.

All: Splash.

Jim: And you had wires from yer Dan Lenos to yer trawl doors, which are two big iron doors weighing about a ton.

Ron: And these are like kites under the water which keep the mouth of the trawl open.

Stan: You clipped yer doors up and lowered them into the water. . .

All: Splash.

Stan: And you were ready to start paying out yer warps.

Jim: Yer warps are two steel hawsers that run from the winch around a set of bollards. The fore warp goes up and through the fore gallows whereas the aft warp runs along the side of the ship, inside of the rail, and up and through the aft gallows.

Ron: And the strain on them warps was tremendous. And if they parted, boy, you'd better not be standing around when it 'appened. They could cut you in 'alf like butter. They could take yer 'ands off, or yer arms off, yer legs off, or even yer 'ead. . .

Stan: Snacker . . . just get on with it, alright?

Ron: Now yer mate and the third 'and 'd be on the winch and they'd pay out yer warps until you come to the first mark, which was a double mark.

Jim: *(On winch.)* Okay skipper.

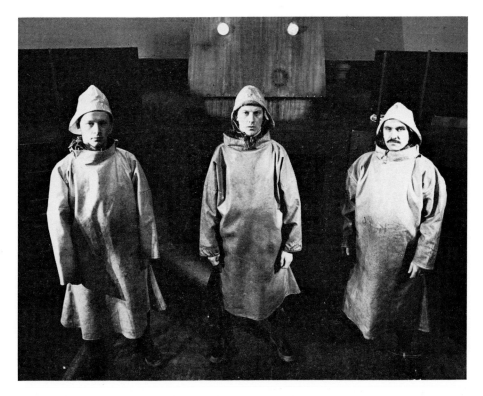

Act 1 Scene 6. Shooting the trawl.

Ted: And you'd build 'er up to full speed, level 'er off to whatever course you want, and shout 'Pay Away.'

Jim makes noise of winch.

Stan: And yer warps 'd be paying out at an 'ell of a speed and the mate has to watch the marks going out and each mark is twenty five fathoms.

Ted: And the rule of thumb you worked on was treble yer length of warp to yer depth of water.

Jim: Coming up, skipper.

Ted: And you'd ease the ship down slow to take the weight off so you could 'ook the messenger on.

Stan: Now yer messenger's an 'ook with a wire on it that runs aft of the towing block and back forrard to the winch. Yer messenger man's got to throw that 'ook over the fore warp, the slack's taken in on the wire, and the 'ook runs down the fore warp, picks up the after warp and brings them in close to the ship's side.

Jim: *(Now as bosun.)* And the bosun's stood at the towing block and as these two warps come up I have to clamp them in the block, and put a pin through to keep them in place.

Ron: And that was a dangerous job 'cos there was no platform or owt, and with the ship 'eaving and rolling those warps could take yer arms off, or even yer 'ead.

Stan and Jim give him a look.

Jim: And until these warps are blocked, the messenger wire which is running round a bollard here is taking all the strain, and if that hook parts which it has done on several occasions, then this wire becomes a whiplash.

Stan: That's why you never stood 'ere, aft of the wire, or between the wire and the centre casing, 'cos if that wire parted, you was bacon. *(Ducks under imaginary wire to the 'safe' position.).*

Jim: And if I wanted a new messenger, I got one. No skipper ever stopped me putting a new one on. It wasn't just my responsibility, it was my life that was at stake.

Ted: But it all 'ad to be done quick like, 'cos time was money, and until you had those warps in the block, you couldn't start fishing.

Jim: *(Putting pin in.)* All square, skipper.

Ron: And away you went.

All: Come ye bold seafaring men, there's fortunes to be made, in the trawling trade.

Ted: Course, after you'd finished towing, you 'ad the whole lot to reverse.

Jim: So it was back to the towing block. Only this time, you've got a long metal bar, a knocking out bar. And what you have to do is, you have to take yer pin out, and knock out the collapsible lip with yer bar. And when these warps come out, boy, do they make some noise.

Ron: And then you 'ove on the winch and up come yer warps. . .

Stan: Up come yer doors. . .

Jim: Up come yer Dan Lenos. . .

Stan: You gets yer codend aboard, you lets go of yer codend. . .

Ron: And out spills yer fish.

Jim: That's if you've got any.

Ted: You always knew when you'd got a good haul, 'cos the codend'd come up before the doors, 'cos as the fish come up out of the depths, their bladders expand and inflate, and the codend'd literally shoot out of the water like a rocket.

Ron: *(Watching imaginary codend.)* Bloody 'ell.

Ted: And I used to watch the deckies' faces and some of 'em looked like they were going to 'ave an 'eart attack at the thought of all that fish they were going to have to gut.

Stan: But sometimes the weight of fish'd be that much, it'd split the net. Then we used to laugh and he'd cry.

Ron: And if the fishing was really bad we used to get all our spare change and chuck it into the sea.

Jim/Ron/Stan: *(Miming throwing coins.)* If we can't catch it, we'll bloody well buy it.

Ted: And we'd blame Father Neptune, we would. People laugh, but to us he was down there below, and if he wanted you to have a bad trip, you got a bad trip.

Stan: My grandad had a bad relationship with Father Neptune. He was a skipper and he'd 'ad a run o' bad luck, and on this particular trip they were just swinging the codend aboard and it split. Instead of the fish landing on the deck, it all went in the water. Well me grandad just stood there, quiet like, and he says to the deckie learner...

Ted: Go down below and get me a bar of tallow.

Ron: You don't mend nets with tallow, skipper.

Ted: Get me a bar of tallow.

Ron: So I goes down below, I gets a bar of tallow and I gave it to him.

Stan: And me grandad goes to the ship's rail and he throws the tallow out as far as he could.

Ted: *(Throws it.)* There you are yer nit-whiskered old bastard, there's the fat to fry it in.

Blackout. They regroup. Maureen enters.

SCENE SEVEN

Maureen: Every Friday we 'ad what we called Fish Dock Races, or Silk Stocking Day. All the wives'd get dolled up and go down the dock to collect their 'usbands' wages.

Jim: 'Cos as deckhands we got paid in two ways. We got a percentage of what the catch made at the market but we also got a basic wage which was paid to our wives while we were at sea.

Maureen: We 'ad a little book like a club card, and we'd queue up, they'd stamp the book, and note down how much they'd give you.

Stan: And we never thought of it as our money, 'cos our wives got it all.

Maureen: And it'd all go on coal and rent and what have you and more often than not, it'd all be gone before he got back. So I'd be off down to 'Uncles' the pawnshop with all his best suits. I tell ya, some of his suits could almost walk to that pawnshop, they could almost jump on the shelf.

Ted: And if you'd had a bad trip, you'd come home and there'd be no settling money at all. Sometimes you even settled in debt. You was owing the company money.

Maureen: So I'd send the kids down the office to try and gerr a sub. 'Me mam's expecting,' they'd say, and the clerk'd say. . .

Jim: Er. . . that's the sixth baby your mother's had this month.

Maureen: But it was disgusting. They'd been slogging their guts out for three weeks and earnt next to nowt. And it was dangerous too. 'Cos their living depended on catching that fish, they used to carry on fishing in weather that they shouldn't a been.

Ron: And if you 'ad an accident and 'ad to be put ashore, your money was stopped. No compensation or owt. An Act of God they called it.

Maureen: It 'appened to my 'usband. He got put ashore and it wasn't owt serious like. So any'ow I goes down to the office and the clerk says. . .

Stan: There'll be no money for you, luv.

Maureen: Well thank you very much. What do you think I live on? Fresh air?

Stan: Go to PAC. They'll help you.

Ted: PAC was Public Assistance. Social Security.

Maureen: Only it wasn't what social security is nowadays, 'cos they 'ad the means test going, and that was a very stringent test indeed.

Jim: (As a Means Test Man.) Knock knock knock. Means Test Man. Let's have a look at yer coalhouse please. Hmm. Pantry. Let's have a look in yer pantry. Aaha. What is this we have here. A piano. There'll be no money for you until you sell that I'm afraid. *(Sniffs.)* Jam, I can definitely smell jam. *(Ferrets around.)*.

Maureen: I'd made a meat pie and with the pastry left over I'd made a few jam tarts.

Jim: *(Whipping off imaginary tablecloth.)* Ahah. Pastry eh? So you can afford to eat pastry eh?

Maureen: We do eat sometimes you know.

Jim: You're one of those that want something for nothing aren't you?

Maureen: The door's there. Out!

Jim: Now just hold yer horses, fishwife.

Maureen: You little rat. And I opens the door and I boots him out. *(Does so.)* Fishwife. I may have been born with a cod in one hand and an 'addock in the other, but I don't take no cheek from no bloody means test man, so there.

Blackout. Others regroup. Maureen exits.

SCENE EIGHT

Stan: Gutting. Nobody used to like gutting.

Jim: Specially if it was small fish, codlings.

Stan: You put yer 'and in yer pocket. You took out yer gutting knife, and you all bent down.

Ron: Sometimes you didn't need to bend down 'cos the fish was up to yer chin.

Stan: It was down, bend yer back, and gut. And you gutted and you gutted and you gutted.

They mime the actions of gutting.

Jim: And when you talk about fish, some people imagine two or three lay there.

Ron: But you could 'ave two or three 'undred baskets.

Stan: What you call a double bag.

Ron: It was all rushed but it were team work.

Jim: If one man missed the whole team was out.

Stan: And you gutted and you gutted and you gutted.

Ron: And the skipper used to leave enough for you so you couldn't get off the deck.

Ted: *(On bridge.)* Call me when you've twenty baskets.

Stan: Don't call 'im. He's only going to tow half an hour.

Jim: Twenty baskets, skipper.

Ted: Pay away.

Ron: There was no stopping.

Stan: All 'e wanted to do was to keep you there, 'cos he was frightened of the gaffers and 'e didn't want to lose 'is job.

Jim: And that's the way fishing's been all the way through. Skippers 'n mates frightened to death of the gaffers, frightened for their jobs. So who got it?

Stan/Jim/Ron: The boys on the deck. *(Continue gutting. Ron falls asleep on his feet.)*.

Ted: *(Hard.)* They all know the success of the trip depends on catching fish. If they couldn't stand it or didn't want to do the work, they wouldn't come aboard. Nobody stands behind 'em with a gun.

Stan: *(Noticing Ron.)* Oi, snacker.

Jim: Eh. He's fallen asleep.

Stan: *(Clouting him.)* Eh.

31

Ron wakes up and starts gutting again. Falls asleep almost immediately.

Ted: Ships can only survive on profit and with millions of pounds invested in these ships, they've gotta show a profit. It's a cut-throat business.

Jim: Eh, he's fallen asleep again. Oi. *(Wakes him up.).*

Stan: I tell you what kid. We'll charge you a tanner every time you fall asleep.

Jim: We'll let you swear though.

Ron: I can't feel me fingers.

Stan: Shut up and gut.

They continue gutting. Ron inevitably falls asleep.

Ted: A skipper's only as good as his last trip. I'm under the threat of sack just the same as they are. If I don't keep poking that fish in, I'm on bloody walkabout.

Stan: Tanner. *(Ron wakes up and struggles to carry on gutting.).*

Ted: It's not easy getting to be skipper. Five years at sea before you can go for yer mate's ticket, two years at sea as mate before you can go for yer skipper's ticket, and then you gotta get a ship. No matter how hard you graft, you can be the best mate in Hull, but until you get that little sign, there's no chance.

Jim: Shilling *(Ron wakes up and continues gutting.).*

Ted: And what you've got to remember is that every other skipper out here is your competitor. If there's a new ship going it's the most successful skipper that gets it. So if they're catching twice as much fish as I am, then I wanna know why. Course they all tell a pack of lies. Oh, I've only got thirty baskets, when what they mean is a hundred and fifty.

Stan: One and six *(Ron wakes up.).*

Ted: It's a struggle. You have to prove yerself and keep proving yerself. You make one mistake and that's you finished after all that flogging you've done.

Jim: Two bob.

Ted: One bloke I knew he was mate on a ship and he got the chance to go skipper. So they calls him up the office and the gaffer says. . .

Maureen: *(As Gaffer.)* See that ship out there. You think you can take her to sea and fill her full of fish?

Ted: I'll do me best, sir.

Maureen: No doubt you'll do your best. At home we have a little pony for the children. Now I could enter that pony for the Derby, and I'm sure it'd do its best. But it wouldn't damn well win. Good morning. *(Maureen exits.).*

Ted: And that was him finished.

Stan: Half a crown.

Ted: It is hard. And you've got to be hard to do it. Where there's two fathoms of salt water, there's no sympathy.

Jim: Three bob.

Ron is increasingly desperate.

Ted: But as the gaffer once said to me, 'A man who likes his job is never a slave to work.'

Ron: *(Screams.)* I wanna go 'ome.

Blackout. They regroup. Lights up quickly.

Stan: One bloke, he'd sailed with me a long time, and he went to the skipper one day and he says...

Ron: I want to go ashore.

Ted: What you talking about? You can't go ashore.

Jim: We were off Bear Island at the time.

Ron: If I can't go ashore, then I'm going to commit suicide.

Ted: Oh, just a minute then.

Stan: And he gave 'im a razor blade.

Ted: Make a good job of it 'cos that's the only way you're going to go ashore.

Blackout. They regroup. Lights back quickly.

Ron: Another time this bloke did actually commit suicide. He jumped overboard. And the mate went up to the skipper and said...

Stan: He's gone. He's jumped over the wall.

Ted: How do you know?

Stan His seaboots are there. And he must have meant it 'cos the towing block's gone. He's used it as a weight.

Jim: And all the skipper said was...

Ted: Bloody 'ell. That was a new towing block that.

Blackout. They regroup. Lights back quickly.

SCENE NINE

Jim: There was no pity in them days. No pity at all.

Stan: We did 40, 50, 60 hours at a time on deck. That's not exaggerating, it's true.

Ted: The skipper's word was law and if he wanted to keep you up, he kept you up.

Ron: I've seen the crew that tired, they just turned into zombies.

Stan: I've seen 'em that tired they've been falling asleep with their 'eads in their soup bowls. You was an 'uman slave, you was killing yourself.

Jim: There's been times after a long spell on deck when you had another six hours watch to do on the bridge. You walked from one side of that bridge to the other just banging yer head against the window to keep yerself awake.

Ron: Ships have been lost because men have been that tired on watch they've just fallen asleep at the wheel.

Stan: And this just went on day after day. It was just accepted.

Jim: You had to be very fit to cope with it. It's not something you just went into, it's something you built up over the years.

Ted: There was some blokes as old as sixty. How the devil they managed it, I just don't know.

Ron: My old man was still at sea at sixty five. 'E 'ad a great big hernia the size of a football and a big steel truss to keep it in. And he was still gutting in the Arctic, at 65, with a bloody big 'ernia.

Jim: And for all this we were classed as casual. Casual labour.

Ron: Can you believe it?

Stan: The most degrading term you can imagine. Casual bloody labour.

Ron: So you've been working 50, 60 odd hours, then God up there says...

Ted: Okay lads, you can knock off for four hours.

Jim: Four hours sleep after sixty hours on deck.

Stan: And you rushed to get yer gear off. You fell in, you just flopped in. You was dead.

They all collapse on the bunks.

Ted: It was the same for the skipper. I've been up three or four days without even taking me boots off. After the initial period you got used to it. You'd 'ave a quick kip and be alright again.

Ron: But they used to do tricks like 'flogging the clock.'

Stan: Aye, instead of giving you four hours, they'd give you three. And the skipper'd shout the mate. . .

Ted: Go and get 'em out.

Stan: So we used to take the ladder away. We'd take it down and the mate'd shout. . .

Ted: Where's that bloody ladder?

Stan: And that way we got another half hour.

Ron: But then you was up, yer gear back on, and back on the freezing deck for another sixty hours.

They stagger out of their bunks.

Ted: I used to get a broom handle, stick it near the bridge window and put me cap on it. That way when they looked up they thought I was still there, and I could 'ave a quick kip without 'em slacking off.

Jim: And yer hands'd be that stiff and sore, you couldn't bear to touch anything. We used to urinate on our hands, yeh, pee on 'em, just to relax them.

Stan: And you got salt water boils on yer wrists, and yer oilfrock was stiff and heavy, and it chafed, and the pain was terrible.

Ron: And you got 'addock rash. Now 'addock rash was a lovely thing.

Jim: When you'd been gutting haddock, all the spawn got between yer fingers, and it chafed until there was bare flesh.

Ron: And when you put 'em in salt water the pain was excruciating.

Stan: And you're on a rolling deck with freezing cold hands and working with very sharp knives.

Jim: And there was no doctor on board. Any problems you went to the skipper.

Ted: Aye, I've done a lot of stitching in my time. A bloke would slip a knife into his arm, he come up on the bridge, I'd put a couple of stitches in it and send him back down again.

Stan: Or maybe frostbite.

Ron: Eh, skipper. I think I've got frostbite in my little fingers.

Ted: I'll soon cure that.

Stan: And he'd get his razor blade out and cut the scabs off his fingers.

Jim: Then he'd get some adhesive tape, black adhesive tape, wrap up his fingers, and send him back down on the deck.

Ted: There, you'll be alright now.

Ron: And bugger me, I 'ad to 'ave a finger off when I gorr 'ome.

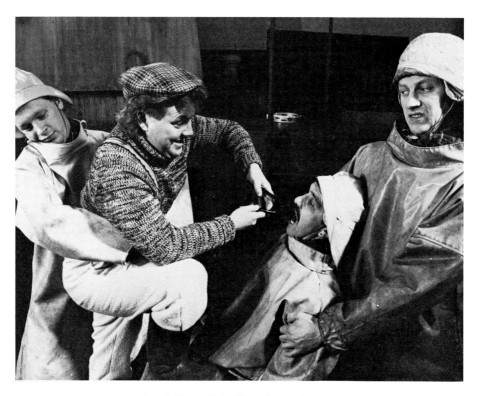

Act 1 Scene 9. Pulling the teeth story.

Ted: I 'ad to be dentist once an' all. This second comes up to me and he says...

Stan: Skipper, can you pull teeth out?

Ted: Aye, course I can. I'd never pulled teeth in me life like, but well you have to have a go at anything don't you?

Stan: It's these two, they'll have to come out like.

Ted: Well, I've no morphine. Just a pair of pincers. Are you sure?

Stan: Yeh.

Ted: Right lads.

Ted comes down onto the deck. Jim gets a chair to sit Stan on. Ron has a pair of pincers. He cleans them on his oilfrock.

Ted: Pincers *(Ron hands them to him.)* Open yer mouth then.

Ron and Jim act as surgeon's assistants. Ted pulls at Stan's mouth. After a struggle the tooth comes out.

Ted: Whisky.

Jim gets a dram and offers it to Stan.

36

Ted: Eh, that's for me. I need that. *(Takes dram and knocks it back.).*

Ted: Are you sure about the other one?

Stan: Yeh.

Another struggle with the pincers. Ron and Jim restrain Stan with arms and legs. Tooth finally comes out.

Ted: *(Handing Stan glass.)* There you go kid. *(Stan knocks it back in one.)* That was to swill yer mouth out.

Stan: Oh. You'd berrer give us another one then.

Grins toothless grin at audience. Blackout. They regroup. Ted back on the bridge.

SCENE TEN

Jim: The weather conditions we worked in. It's almost beyond human description.

Ron: The wind'd be that fierce you'd get frostbite on yer face.

Stan: You could hardly look into the weather 'cos your eyeballs couldn't stand the cold.

Jim: Yer feet'd be frozen into yer boots.

Ron: Yer mittens'd be lumps of ice.

Stan: As the nets came out the water the ice'd be forming solid across the meshes.

Ron: The fish'd fall out frozen onto the deck. You couldn't even get a knife into 'em.

Jim: Seas'd be coming at you big as houses. And when she stuck her rail under, she stuck it under.

Stan: The sea'd come aboard solid, hit the casing behind you, spurt up and wash you off yer feet.

Ron: The whole crew'd be washed along the deck, floundering under water.

Ted: And from the bridge you'd see nothing, maybe a rail and you'd think, Christ, is she gonna come back?

Jim: And you'd be hearing telegraphs going, and gradually she'd come up and clear herself of water.

Stan: And you'd pick yourself up, check you was all there, and carry on fishing.

Ron: 'Cos some skippers wouldn't stop even if there was a bloody gale blowing.

Ted: Meself I never pushed it. If it came on to blow, I got the gear in and ran for shelter. But some skippers, especially the younger ones, they're out to make a name for themselves. Their fear of failure was greater than their fear of the sea. And boy, did they take some risks.

The lights fade. Bridge lights fade up from backstage silhouetting the actors. FX: Sound of wind and sea. Ted is on the bridge. Ron, Stan and Jim are gutting. They have to shout to be heard.

Ron: Oi.

Jim: What?

Ron: Yer face.

Jim: What?

Ron: You've got scabs on yer face.

Jim: So have you.

Ron: What?

Jim: Christ. We've all got bloody frostbite.

Ted: *(Bawling.)* Two minutes to hauling.

Stan: Haven't you had enough?

They break to various positions. Ron is at the fore gallows. Jim is at the towing block. Stan is on the winch.

Ron: Look out.

FX: Crashing wave. Strobe light reveals the men being battered and thrown across the decks. Sound of wave dies. Bridge lights back on.

Jim: It threw me up onto the casing and even there the water was up to my neck and I thought, Christ, somebody'll have gone there.

Stan: I 'ad. I went straight over the port side but the backwash swept me back.

Ron: *(Screaming.)* Water.

FX: Crashing wave. Strobe. The men are thrown about. Sound dies. Bridge lights back.

Ted: Get the gear in, we're going for Ritterhook.

Jim: About time, you stupid bastard.

Jim mimes knocking out the warps. FX: Menacing twang followed by the sound of the winch and then the doors crashing against the bows.

Ron: The independant's stuck.

Stan: Use the jilson.

Jim: Bugger the jilson, just get it off.

Ron leans over tugging at imaginary wire. He suddenly screams and freezes. Sound of wind is cut. Snap spot on Ron.

Ron: *(Calm but in a state of shock.)* Me 'and was caught in the door. All I could feel was the sense of something crunching in me glove. It was a weird feeling. And every time the ship rolled it pulled me 'and further in. The only way to get it out was to heave on the gear and as the warps came onto the winch I pulled me 'and out. By this time me mitten was in ribbons. Me glove and me 'and was torn to shreds. I took me glove off, turned it upside down, and what was left of me finger fell out. They put me 'and in a bowl of flour, and surprisingly there was very little blood. I was lucky. It could have taken me life.

Full lights up.

Stan: And for what? A few seconds saved and a few more fish in the pounds.

Jim: And that's how these ships were bought. Blood money and a reckless disregard for the safety and welfare of the crew.

Ron: The skipper was god. The mate was undergod. And an accident, well that was just an Act of God.

Ted: It was an adventure. And you all had a share in it.

Music for trawlermen's shanty starts over:

Stan: I suppose he's right. You see we always thought we were gonna make the big money. So we never bothered with trade unions or inequality, 'cos we were the boys who were going to the top.

Jim: Unions are for poor people. Me, I'm going to be Paul Getty.

Ron: And when you've been away for three weeks and you've only got a couple of days on shore, who the hell wants to go to a union meeting?

Stan: So we closed our eyes to what really happened. The corruption, the injustice, and the accidents.

Jim: We used to say that if you got swept over board, the best thing you could do was to get to the bottom and run like hell for the shore.

Ron: And you 'ad to laugh 'cos it might be your turn next trip.

Stan: You see fishing was one big gamble. And the biggest gamble of all was when you went out that dock whether you was gonna come back or not.

Maureen enters.

Jim: And at sea there were just three things you looked forward to — sleep, food, and getting back home to yer wife and kids.

TRAWLERMENS SHANTY

We're homeward bound, we're homeward bound
Goodbye fare ye well, goodbye fare ye well
We're saying goodbye to the old fishing grounds
Hurrah me boys, we're homeward bound.

Goodbye to you Dogger and Bear Island too
Goodbye fare ye well, goodbye fare ye well
Black ice and foul weather it's goodbye to you
Hurrah me boys, we're homeward bound.

Goodbye to you Greenland I know you right well
Goodbye fare ye well, goodbye fare ye well
There's times you've been grand and there's time you've been hell
Hurrah me boys, we're homeward bound.

You'll give us good catches and show us fair play
Goodbye fare ye well, goodbye fare ye well
And send a good man to the bottom next day
Hurrah me boys, we're homeward bound.

We're homeward bound we'll have you to know
Goodbye fare ye well, goodbye fare ye well
And straight up the 'Umber to Kingston we'll go
Hurrah me boys, we're homeward bound.

We'll taste every pleasure of life on the shore
Goodbye fare ye well, goodbye fare ye well
For the North Sea is waiting to claim us once more
Hurrah me boys, we're homeward bound.

We'll laugh and we'll fight and we'll clown and we'll cry
Goodbye fare ye well, goodbye fare ye well
We'll drink every boozer on 'Essle Road dry
Hurrah me boys, we're homeward bound. Homeward bound.

INTERVAL

PHOTOGRAPHS OF A VOYAGE BY THE TRAWLER "ARSENAL"

The following series of photographs illustrating the trawling process were taken in the 1950's by a "Grimsby Evening Telegraph" staff photographer aboard the oil-burning trawler "Arsenal," working from Grimsby.

(Top) Taken from the bridge, "en route" for the fishing grounds.

(Bottom) Cow hides being fixed with lashings to the cod ends to prevent them being chafed on the sea bed.

44

(Right) Cod ends being wired prior to paying away.

(Below) On the bridge before shooting. Five degrees to starboard.

Coming round on the cables ready for shooting. One man on starboard brake, one on port brake.

Doors already out; now ready to shoot trawl.

Mending a few scale holes before letting go the cod ends. The net is attached to the drum by the jilson wire.

(Top) Putting chain in after door prior to hawling in the net. After door comes up before fore door.

(Bottom) Hauling top part of net aboard. Top wings are visible.

48

With part of the net already aboard, pulling back on the belly, or "snotlering up," to close the ends of the belly together.

Heaving tight on the belly to overhaul the trawl.

Pulling out the cod ends prior to tying up. By the amount of fish visible, a slack haul.

51

Gutting while still towing. The warps are visible.

(Top) Gutting squad at work. After gutting, fish go via the washer into the after-fish room.

(Bottom) The decks were cleaned with chloride of lime or sand, then washed down with sea water. The pump visible in the picture was called a "donkey."

"Steaming" for home or to fresh fishing grounds.

Coming into Grimsby fish dock. The tug only takes the ship in, not out. The crew are already in their ashore togs.

(Top) Coming alongside other trawlers in the fleet.

(Bottom) "Lumpers" at Grimsby fish dock sorting the fish by size for the buyers.
They were known as "Bobbers" in Hull.

55

ACT TWO

SCENE ONE

The actors take up positions. They are dressed as 'lumpers.'

ANOTHER MORNING

Jim:
Six of a clock and a new day dawning
I'd lie in my warm white bed alone
Hear the swish of the tyres and the cycling men
And the rattle of the milk on the doorside stone
On another morning.

Jim/Stan:
Frost on the pane and the street lamps yellow
Door slams loud in the winter air
Listen for the click of the clog irons come
Down the long street and across the square
On another morning.

Jim/Stan/Ron:
Turn of the key and I know he's with me
Back from the night that I could not know
From the steaming breath and the shouting men
And the arc lights bright on the trampled snow
On another morning.

Jim/Stan/Ron:
And the fire leaps high with a laugh and a roaring
The tea's hot and strong and the bones soon thaw
And I creep down the stair to the warm belonging
The joy of the old man home once more
On another morning.

Jim:
Lie in your bed hear the new day rising
But know in your heart that it's not the same
As your dreams drift on to the old dead days
And remember the times when the clog irons came.

All:
On another morning.

57

Music starts for:

LUMPER'S LIFE

All:
The fish is waiting in the hold, the nights upon the town
Folk with sense are in their beds but the lumpers they go down
Down Pneumonia Jetty where the wind cuts like a knife
I wish to Christ I'd never started on the lumper's life.

Chorus:
And it's all the night and half the day
Sweating for your lumper's pay
Fill the boxes, lump 'em down
Lumping's hard in Grimsby Town.

Stan:
We're called the midnight millionaires by folk who never know
How yer hands go stiff encased in ice when the temperature's below
The wind cuts through yer guts me lads and yer face is stiff and blue
And you wish the trawler owners were down there instead of you.

Chorus

Jim:
Me dad he was a lumper, a dockman all his life
Me mother told me sister never be a lumper's wife
You'll wash his fishy overalls and darn his stiff old socks
And every night you'll sleep alone while he goes down the docks.

Chorus

Ron:
If ever I win the pools me lads me lumping days are through
I'll cash me cheque from Littlewoods and I know just what I'll do
I'll treat me mates and say goodbye and leave the lumping life
And then I'll go to bed at night and get to know me wife.

Chorus

All:
I'll burn me dirty clogs and throw me lumping card away
Shove me leggings in the shed and leave 'em there to stay
I'll tell the lousy setter on to stuff his midnight call
And turn me back forever on the bloody cold North Wall.

Chorus and end.

Maureen: They were lumpers in Grimsby, but in 'Ull they was bobbers.

Jim   We started at two in the morning and in winter time the job was hard and cruel.

Ron: You was wide open to the elements, snow, ice, freezing conditions.

Stan: But the pay was good. We was on two quid a day when the average labourer was gerring six quid a week.

Ted: You allus worked in gangs, and yer gang consisted of...

Ron: Four below men.

Stan: A swinger.

Jim: A weighman.

Ted: A winchman.

Maureen: And barrer lads.

They break into their various positions and roles.

Ron: Now yer belowman was below deck and we 'ad to put all the fish into a basket, and we 'ad a bobbing 'ook which you smashed the ice with, stabbed the fish in the 'ead and put 'em into the basket. And it's all different sizes and all different sorts, and the art is to get all the same size into the same basket.

Ted: The winchman was on the quay, and I've got a rope going from me winch up to a jin wheel on the mast of the ship, then down below decks with an 'ook on the end to 'ang the basket.

Stan: And the swinger, I'm on the deck, and depending on how I sets me jin wheel makes a difference to the whole operation. If I sets it right, I make it easy for meself and the weighman.

Jim: 'Cos I'm stood here ready to catch that basket at the end of its momentum and tip it into a kit, which is a big metal drum like a dustbin.

Maureen: And the kit's standing on a scale, and when there's ten stonner in that kit, me the barrer lad takes it off the scale and to where it's got to go.

Ted: So I've got the drum of me winch revolving and it's going really fast and if I pull back on the end of me rope I can govern the speed and leverage on the basket.

Ron: And up it goes. Pull up.

Stan: And I've got to swing this basket weighing anything from ten to fifteen stone with the ease of a tennis player playing tennis.

Jim: And I've got to catch that basket and that's where his skill comes in again, 'cos he's got to judge the swing and hold the weight of it on his rope so I can empty it.

Maureen: So there's a lot of skill involved between the three men transferring the basket from the 'atch to the quay, to the kit.

Ron: And with a trawler you're talking anywhere between five hundred and four thousand kit depending on what sort of trip they'd 'ad. Pull up. *(Sees basket up.)*.

Stan: *(Swinging the basket.)* Red Army.

Jim: *(Receiving the basket.)* Red Army.

Ron: Pull up.

Stan: *(Swinging.)* Craven Park.

Jim: *(Receiving.)* Craven Park.

Maureen: Now as you might have gathered, there's a bit of jargon in all of this.

Ted: As the swinger was swinging the fish ashore he'd shout out instructions to the weighman as to what sort of fish he was getting.

Ron: And every swinger would 'ave 'is own way o' saying things and him and the weighman would have their own little vocabulary.

Stan: Redfish would be 'all reds' or 'red army' or 'sowdiers.'

Jim: Dogfish'd be 'dogs' or 'Craven Park' 'cos of the dogtrack.

Maureen: And there'd be a whole repartee going between 'em.

Ron: Pull up.

Stan: Coal for yer 'ole.

Jim: Coal for yer 'ole.

Ron: Pull up.

Stan: Coal for money.

Jim: Coal for money.

Ron: Now coal was colefish see, and there's a connotation from the old days when the coalman would drop a bag of coal in for the missus in return for sexual favours. And o' course if he wanted paying in money, not sex, he'd shout, 'Coal for money.'

Ted: And one morning we comes off the dock and them two 'ad been shouting 'Coal for money' and we goes past this woman stood on her doorstep on Liverpool Street...

Stan: It's about seven in the morning and we're all clomping past in our clogs on our way 'ome...

Jim: And she says to us...

Maureen: Who was that silly sod trying to sell coal all night? Who wants to buy coal in the middle of the night?

Stan: We wus wetting ourselves.

Jim: And you could never keep a secret on the dock. There was this bloke and he was a foreman and he'd just been to see the pictures the night before. It was the talkies, sound had just come in. And he comes down the dock the next day and he's telling everybody about it and he's real excited.

Ron: Hey lads, you should 'ave seen those wolves. You should have 'eard 'em. They were going 'Whooooo.' All these wolves like. They were, I'm telling you, they were going Whoooooooo.

Jim: So the next day he's down the dock again, and there's twenty ships all in a row. And he has to start at one end and walk the whole length of twenty ships. And as he's going past every single bobber on every ship is going...

Jim/Stan/Ted: Whooooo . . . whoooooo.

Stan: Another fellow, Scarborough Ray we called 'im, lived down 'Arrow Street. And he'd just 'ad a bath purr in his own house, and for the first time in his life he's having a bath in 'is own house. *(Ted does all the actions.)* And next door there was another bobber in the yard, and there's Scarborough Ray sat in 'is bath and he shouts out to his wife...

Ted: Can you 'ear me splashing Gladys? Can you 'ear me splashing?

Stan: And the same thing next day. Twenty ships all in a row and every bobber shouting...

Stan/Jim/Ron: Can you 'ear me splashing Gladys? Can you 'ear me splashing?

Ted: And I got that every morning for the next thirty years of me life.

Stan: I tell you it was one big laugh down the dock. It was a cold wet job but you'd be amazed at the 'appiness and 'umour.

Ron: The thing about bobbing was your day's work was there. You 'ad yer ship, the amount of fish in it, and the sooner you gorr it finished, the sooner you gorr 'ome.

LUMPER'S LIFE *(Reprise)*

All:
The fish is waiting in the hold the night's upon the town
Folk with sense are in their beds but the lumpers they go down
Down Pneumonia Jetty where the wind cuts like a knife
I wish to Christ I'd never started on the lumper's life.

And it's all the night and half the day
Sweating for yer lumper's pay
Fill the boxes, lump 'em down, lumping's hard in Grimsby Town.

All exit except Maureen.

SCENE TWO

Maureen: The men on the fish dock, they were great. They were rough but they were really good. And o' course they all lived down 'Essle Road. I 'ad a doctor's street guide, and if you looked down the list, the names and addresses and occupations, you'd see that the whole area was connected with fishing. It was a community all of its own.

And 'Essle Road was a road to be proud of, it was. You could go anywhere in England and somebody would always remember one road and that'd be 'Essle Road. And it was a mass of shops. There was Liptons, World Stores, Home & Colonial, Boyes, Europe Stores. And it was all personal service. People were helpful, they were friendly, they'd go out their way to 'elp you. You could go to any fisherman's house, cup o' tea, the kettle was always on.

And living down a terrace, I mean we practically lived on each other's doorsteps. And we all knew what was going on. And if a baby was born with a veil all the other wives would come round to 'ave a look. You see a baby born with a veil was meant to be good luck, it meant he could go to sea 'nd never ever be lost. What it was was a piece of skin hanging over the face, and the midwife'd cut it off and o' course you kept it. And all the other wives'd want it. You could have sold it for a fortune. 'Oh give it to me, Moo, I'll give you a 'undred pounds, let me 'ave it.' But o' course you didn't part with it, it was priceless.

And we all used to braid nets down the terraces as well. You'd take your window off, put your net across it and work it out on the terrace. And was they 'eavy. I 'ad 'em all over my house. I 'ad 'em on the stairs, in the living room, kitchen, front room, I tell you, my 'ouse looked like a fish dock all on its own. But I kept it smart. Especially when your 'usband was coming 'ome. Down come yer curtains, up come yer mats, off come yer bedclothes, and we'd 'ave a good old washday. 'Cos I never used to wash when they went away to sea. It was taboo. It was like you were washing them away forever. But everything 'ad to be just so for 'em coming 'ome. I'd be off down the pawnshop for 'is best suits, and all 'is clothes'd be laid out ready for 'im going out that first night with 'is mates. 'Cos I never went out with 'im that first night 'ome. Are you ready?

All: *(Off.)* Aye, we're ready.

Ron, Stan, Jim and Ted enter in their best suits, ties and grease-backed hair.

SCENE THREE

Stan: A fisherman was always in fashion. We always bought the best.

Jim: Ruck back suit.

Ted: Padded shoulders.

Ron: Wide lapels.

Jim: Half moon pockets.

Stan: And a tie with a very small knot in it.

Ted: Always wore white shirts. Wouldn't go out without a clean white shirt.

Ron: And a Boston Bang 'aircut, with loads o' Brylcream.

Maureen: You'd see 'em rolling down 'Essle Road with their best suits on, and the pockets'd be bulging with saveloys and cowheels.

Stan: We'd gerra a pork pie *(with gestures.)*. Slice the top off. And fill it with tomato sauce. Shove the top back on. *(They take a bite.)*.

All: Luvly.

Maureen: A fisherman just stood out. They always looked like they'd just got off an 'orse. They stood with their legs wide apart.

Ted: And stood at a bar, the bar'd be rocking a bit.

Jim: It does that after ten pints.

Ted: Well yeh, but it was because you'd been on a rolling deck for three weeks, and that's how you kept your balance.

Stan: If you landed early morning tide, you'd be down the dock same day for your settling money.

Jim: And if you'd had a good trip, you'd have a fistful of fivers to spend, and spend it you did.

Ted: First stop off'd be a pint with the lads. Probably make a whole day of it. Do the whole o' Hessle Road.

Ron: Once I 'ad a pint, you know, I couldn't care less. I once did 'Ull and Grimsby. I did the Rats Nest, the 'Umber, the Lincoln, the Barrel. And I think I ended up in London. I were paralytic.

Maureen: Some of 'em got that drunk they'd wake up back aboard the ship and they didn't even know they'd been 'ome.

Stan: But most of us, second day, we'd treat the wives. Take 'em out, do the whole town. It was like an 'oneymoon every three weeks.

Ted: And it was always taxis with fishermen. Even if you were just going up the street you'd take a taxi.

Jim: 'Cos time was valuable, see. You only had two, three days at home at the most, so you weren't going to waste valuable time hanging about at bus stops.

Maureen: But we gorr a lot of stick from people that weren't fishermen. Ooh look at them always out boozing, always got loads of money, always enjoying themselves. We got a lot of that sort of thing.

Ron: But that was the way of life. We 'ad three weeks rough, so when you come 'ome, you enjoyed yourself.

Maureen: And fishermen were generous, they were. The kids'd follow 'em down street and shout 'Give us a tanner, mister.' And they'd put their 'ands in their pocket, and any loose change, silver, whatever, they'd throw it on the street for the kids.

Stan: And if anyone was out of a ship, we'd treat 'em. We kept each other going. The company didn't keep yer going. It was a very close community that looked after its own.

The men break and sit at the table drinking. They each put a fiver in one of the empty glasses for a kitty.

Maureen: That first day 'ome they'd be in the boozer with their mates gerring legless. And they'd all be talking about fishing. Wharr 'ad 'appened on the trip, how much they'd got. And some of them stories, you just wouldn't believe 'em. But they was true stories. Every single one of 'em was true.

Jim: Did I tell you about this bloke. He was on a ship with me. And he was crazy about knives, absolutely crazy about this collection of knives. Always played the hard man, that sort of kid. Anyway he says to me this trip, 'Let's play a trick on the deckie learner, show him a thing or two. Hey Jock, I'll tell you what we'll do, you put this block of wood up your oilfrock, up yer back right, and I'll come at you from behind with this knife, in the block of wood, and he'll think I've stabbed you.' Right. Fair enough. So we got it all set up. I'm at one side with the block o' wood up me frock, and he's at the other, knife in his hand. And he comes screaming across ... Ooojah ... into the block o' wood, and I'm lying there going ugh, ugh on the deck, you know dying away. And the deckie learner, he's standing like this, eyes popping out of his head, he didn't believe it. But the thing was nobody had thought of telling the skipper about this. And the skipper's there on the bridge watching all this. So what does he do? He takes one jump off the bridge, onto the deck. Breaks both his bloody ankles.

Ted: I knew this bloke, right? He was a great dancer. Anywhere we were, he'd get up and give it a jig around. This was years before you 'ad yer disco dancing. But he was sort of like yer John Travolta of his age. Anyway one day we're in the pub, with the wireless and my mate's up dancing...

Stan: Show us, go on.

Ted: No.

All: Go on.

Ted: I'm not very good at it, mind. So the wireless is on and he's dancing away. *(Does wild disco dancing.)*. Giving it loads of welly... Then the music stops. Well, he's caught in mid air isn't he, dead embarrassed. Doesn't know what to do. There's an iron stanchion in front of him. So what does he do? He turns round and punches it. Fractures his bloody wrist. We had to take him off to hospital. Crazy.

Ron: Hey, did I tell you about old Dillinger last week?

Stan: Bloody 'ell, Dillinger.

Ron: You know the bloke that comes down the docks with the fishermen's bags... he came down this one morning, parks his horse outside the gate, and gets the bags and takes 'em down to the lads. Dillinger comes along and sees this horse and cart and thinks, hello, we'll have a joke here. So he unshackles the horse, takes it through the gate, puts the shafts through the gate and fastens it back on the cart. Not satisfied with this, he gets an old souwester, cuts a couple of 'oles in it and put it on the horse's 'ead. Then he gets a couple o' clumpers and puts 'em on the horse's feet, so the poor bloody 'orse is stood there, with an 'at on its 'ead, clumpers on its feet, and its shafts through the gate. Well the bloke comes back, he takes one look at it and says 'How the bloody 'ell did it manage that?'

Stan: He did summat else an' all. He was coming down 'Essle Road one day and he'd been on the beer and he gets to Woolies. And he sees all the bairns outside in the prams. And he was a real soft hearted kid wasn't he? And he sees this bairn in this shitty old pram. So he takes the bairn out the shitty pram and puts it in a posh one. Takes the posh bairn out and puts it in the shitty pram. And then he thinks Oh I'll swop a few more round. Swops a black un for a white un, then the mothers came out of Woolies. Well there was hell to play. 'That's not my bairn.' 'What's that bairn doing in my pram?' So they called the police and poor old Dillinger got arrested.

Maureen: I've got one an' all. My dad used to be an engineer. And he got a lot of stick off the deckies.

Ron: You don't work in engine room. Not like us on deck.

Maureen: So me dad'd say back.

Ted: When did you last burn your arse on a trip?

Maureen: Anyow one night they all got blind drunk and they 'ad a row about how the winches worked. So they goes 'ome, goes into the kitchen, and starts trying to explain what they were saying with the mangle.

Jim is the mangle. Ron, Stan and Ted are drunk.

Ted: Right then, get rolling, kid.

Ron operates the mangle. Jim's arms are the rollers.

Now the danger with ... pay attention man ... The danger with winches is ... you've got to watch yer fingers, you gotta watch you don't get yer fingers caught in it...

Stan: The danger with winches is you've gotta mind you don't get yer 'ead in 'em. *(Tries to shove Ted's head in the winch.)*.

Ted: No it's yer fingers you've got to watch ... Aarrgh ... it's got me finger.

Maureen: And me dad got his finger trapped in the mangle.

Ted: Aarrgh ...

65

Act 2 Scene 3. Pub yarns.

Maureen: And it took it off. Yeh. He'd worked on trawlers all his life and he goes and loses his finger in the bloody mangle.

They regroup. Ted and Maureen are sitting as in a bar. Stan and Jim are either side of the stage.

Jim: I was in the Subway Club this time, and this bloke comes in and he's always complaining about the beer.

Stan: This beer's flat.

Jim: So the barman thinks, I've had enough of this guy. I'm going to sort him out once and for all. So what does he do? He gets some Epsom Salts and puts it into the beer.

Stan: That's the best bloody pint I've ever 'ad in 'ere.

Jim: So this goes on all over lunch time. So after a few pints, aye you've guessed it, the Epsom Salts starts to take effect.

Stan: Oooh, I'll have to have a shit.

Rushes over to stool.

Jim: So he rushes off to the toilet and makes it just in time.

Stan: Oooh.

Jim: But unfortunately, and this is the sad bit, there was no toilet paper.

Stan: There's no bloody toilet paper in 'ere. Can somebody gerr us some?

Jim: So one of the lads nips round to the newsagents and gets back in two minutes flat.

Ron: I've got some.

Stan: Sling it over then.

Ron: Righto.

Pours a packet of confetti over Stan.

Stan: Bloody 'ell.

They regroup.

Maureen: I'll tell you about this other time. Me and me 'usband had gone for a drink, and one of shipmates comes in, so they decide to go off and have a drink together, leaving me on me own. Well it gets to closing time and I has to leave, and it 'ad come in real foggy. So I gets on the tram and gets off at Liverpool Street, and I thought I'll wait for 'im to turn up. Three trams later.

Jim: Ting ting.

Ted: Ting ting.

Stan: Ting ting.

Maureen: He finally turns up. Drunk as hell. He didn't have a leg to stand on. *(Ron is the drunk husband staggering along on the first level.)* So I thought I'll follow him, see where he goes. So we goes up 'Essle Road...

Jim, Ted and Stan make traffic noises. Ron staggers about as if in the middle of the road. Does a V sign at the traffic.

Maureen: And we goes down 'Essle Road. *(Same as before. Ron nearly gets run over.)* And he doesn't know where he is, or what he's doing, and finally we gets to the railway line on Hawthorne Avenue and bang... *(Ron does a pratt fall.)* Down he goes. But the beauty of it was, he's lying on the pavement and he's trying to wrap the flagstones round him 'cos he thinks he's in bed.

Ron: Eh, give us some lapping, luv, it in't half cold.

Maureen: Anyow this bloke comes along and he says...

Stan: What's the matter, luv, have you dotted him?

Maureen: I wish I could bloody dot 'im. It's me 'usband.

Stan: Oh, sorry.

Maureen: Anyow him and this other bloke they gets him up and they gets him 'ome. And he doesn't know where he is or what he's doing. *(Ted and Stan help Ron down from the upper level and seat him in a chair. Ron lolls over the table.)* And he was supposed to be sailing that morning. So I thought, I'll give him the treatment. *(Jim does the actions with the mug.)* I gets a big mug o' black coffee, puts a big knob o' washing soda into it and gives it to him. Well, I don't know what it does to the lining of the stomach but usually it sobers him up. *(Ron drinks and promptly throws up.)* Only this time he still didn't know which ship he was sailing on. So I gets the pram out. *(Jim wheels on pram. Stan and Ted bundle Ron onto it.)* With a bit of heaving and pulling I manages to gerr 'im into the pram. And the pram's creaking and groaning, and his head is lolling out of one end and his feet are lolling out the other, and finally I gets him to the dock, bundles him up the gangplank, sea bag, mattress and all, and onto the ship.

Stan: And there was a big superstition about wives not seeing their 'usbands off to sea. It was like the washing. If you waved 'em goodbye, you waved 'em goodbye forever.

Maureen: I tell ya. If I'd 'ave been superstitious about that, he'd 'ave never gorr off to sea.

Ron: It's me last trip. I'm never going again.

Maureen: Oh shut up and sing the bloody song.

Ted plays guitar. Jim harmonica. Maureen and Stan exit. Ron sings the song from the pram.

THE BIONIC FISHERMAN

Oh me name is Henry Hawkins, I'm a trawlerman of fame
From Fleetwood to the Faroes all the deckies know me name
So listen to me story and I'll tell you if I can
How I became the nation's first bionic fisherman.

We were halfway up the 'Umber when I started my career
A lump fell off the bridge and caught me right behind the ear
Me lughole dropped off on the deck and lay there all alone
Till the third 'and shouted 'What's this ere?,' which caused a mighty groan.

So it's straight to the infirmary they took me speedily
And when the surgeon saw me well he rubbed his hands with glee
Says he we've got technology a working on our side
And an electronic earole can be very soon supplied.

So within a fortnight I was back upon the briny deep
And my bionic earole soon began to earn its keep
I could 'ear a codfish fart me lads and spot a shrimp that snored
And the skipper went and threw the echo sounder overboard.

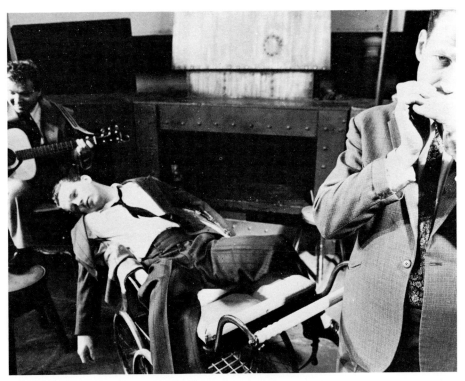

Act 2. "The Bionic Fisherman."

And the next trip that I got me lads the skipper was a clown
He'd listen to the football match while trawling up and down
And as the nets came o'er the side he shouted 'Town have scored'
And me legs got squashed to jelly between a two ton otter board.

So they radioed a chopper and they took me to the shore
And straight to the infirmary all spouting blood and gore
The surgeon rushed to greet me with his doctors in a swarm
Saying 'Hello Henry, welcome back, we've kept your bedpan warm.'

And with a bit of micro surgery my legs were fit as fleas
With twin hydraulic ankles and a steel spring in me knees
And the first thing that I did me lads when I got back on deck
Was to kick the skipper up the bum and he landed in Quebec.

They promoted me to skipper then within a week or two
I was Britain's champion arse-kicker, well what else could they do?
I 'ad me ship, I 'ad me crew and I was doing fine
Till I went and caught me goolies in a loop of towing line.

Well me heart was filled with sorrow as we came in sight of land
I was thinking melancholy thoughts of Henry's final stand
Till the doctor said cheer up me lad and get up off your back
For although you've lost yer knackers lad, you haven't lost the knack.

Well atomic powered wedding tackle's just the thing for me
The word got round among the girls while I was out at sea
And blow me down the very next time me ship came into dock
There's a line of eager ladies waiting half way round the block.

Oh me name is Henry Hawkins, I'm a trawlerman of fame
From Grimsby up to Aberdeen the tarts all know me name
Wherever I may shoot my trawl I'm always in demand
For the ladies all love Henry, the bionic fisherman.

Ron collapses. Blackout. Smoke starts pouring onstage, during the scene change. The actors regroup with Jim as the enquiry chairman seated at the table centre. Sound of wind and sea.

Ted: *(From the bridge.)* We are going over. We are laying over. Help me.

FX: Crashing sea. The sound fades. The bridge lights fade up lighting the actors from behind through the dense smoke.

SCENE FOUR

Jim: *(As the enquiry chairman. He speaks in measured tones but not without emotion.)* The St. Romanus sailed from Hull on the early afternoon of the tenth of January 1968 bound for the Icelandic fishing grounds, and manned by a crew of twenty hands all told including a radio operator.

Maureen: I didn't believe it. I just couldn't believe he wasn't coming home.

Jim: The Kingston Peridot sailed from Hull on the tenth of January 1968 bound for the Norwegian fishing grounds, manned by a crew of twenty hands all told. The crew did not include a radio operator, but the skipper had a radio telegraphy certificate.

Maureen: Even to this day I still sometimes think he might be alive somewhere. That one day he'll just walk in through the door and tell me what really happened.

Jim: The Ross Cleveland sailed from Hull on the morning of the twentieth of January bound for the Icelandic fishing grounds and manned by a crew of twenty hands all told.

Stan: If you can imagine a ship, especially a mere trawler of three or four hundred tons, the whole superstructure is covered in two feet of pure ice. And it attracts more water, more ice, and it freezes, and the ships become top heavy and they just turn tail. There's no way of surviving. There's no way out, no back door or owt.

Jim: The first mate of the Icelandic trawler Vikingur III reported that about 18.30 GMT on the 11th of January, he heard a Mayday call.

Ted: Mayday, mayday, mayday. This is the British trawler St. Romanus from Hull.

Ron: It's like a mist comes off the water. The air is that colder, it's more or less colder than the water. So as the spray comes aboard it freezes, as it sprays so it turns to ice. There's wires, inch wires, that'll go to about two foot 'cause it's freezing that hard.

Jim: On the morning of the 26th of January the Kingston Peridot had a conversation with the Kingston Sardius. It was arranged to resume contact in the evening after the evening weather report had been sent in. The weather at Kiolsen Bank however deteriorated and the radio operator of the Kingston Sardius was unable to make contact with the Kingston Peridot and although he continued to attempt to establish such communication until about one o'clock the next morning, he never succeeded.

Maureen: The first time they came there was a knock on the door and there was just two men dressed in dark suits and they asked me if I wanted to pray.

Ron: Ice attracts more ice, and it just builds up and builds up until eventually it's out of control.

Ted: We're going over. I am laying over. Help me.

Stan: The only way round it, which is pitiful really, was to get the men on deck with their axes and chop it by hand. It was something you had to do. You had to make an effort even though it was futile.

Jim: On the 29th of January an inflatable but partly deflated life raft identified as belonging to the Kingston Peridot was found on the east coast of Axarfiord, and it was seen that there was a lot of oil on the sea and a number of seabirds were covered with oil.

Maureen: They visited me three times in all. Twice to ask me if I wanted to pray and the third time to ask me about the stone they were going to lay for each man in the new fishermen's bethel. It was about twenty pounds and I couldn't afford it. I didn't have the money and I think they thought I didn't care, and that worried me. I didn't want anybody to think I didn't care. I just didn't have the money.

Jim: In the opinion of the court the probable cause of the loss of the Kingston Peridot was that the vessel capsized due to loss of stability in the conditions experienced. This enquiry demonstrates the necessity for the investigation of the stability of trawlers, particularly those fishing in Arctic waters.

Church organ starts at low level – 'Abide With Me.'

Maureen: At the service at Holy Trinity Church, nobody said a word. We all just filed in and filed out. It was like the Lord Mayor's Parade. I didn't feel sad. I didn't feel anything.

Jim: In the afternoon of the 3rd of February a bad weather forecast was received and the skipper of the Ross Cleveland determined to seek shelter. A

71

Act 2 Scene 4. The '68 Disasters.

considerable number of other trawlers were fishing in the same neighbourhood and they also determined to seek shelter, most of them in the same fiord as the Ross Cleveland.

Maureen: The minister read out each name one by one. There was a lot of names to read out. I nearly missed my dad's name. I could hardly hear 'cause I was sitting at the back.

Jim: At about 23.30 on the 4th of February, due to ice on the scanner, the Ross Cleveland was unable to use her radar. The trawler Kingston Andalusite which was close by to starboard of her was asked to pass information obtained from her radar to the Ross Cleveland and agreed to do so.

Maureen: It was just a big show for the press and people to gawp at us. It wasn't for us. It wasn't for the men.

Jim: Some ten minutes later, at about 23.40 hours, just as the Ross Cleveland's radar had got back into operation again, the Ross Cleveland and the Kingston Andalusite, which had been laid with the wind on her starboard side, determined to get head to wind and dodge across to the eastern side of the fiord in order to avoid being set aground on the western side.

Maureen: He was a survivor. I was sure he'd find a way of getting out.

Jim: With her wheel hard a-starboard and with engines working at half speed, the skipper of the Ross Cleveland endeavoured to bring his vessel head into the wind. She however failed to respond. The engines were run full speed ahead and the Ross Cleveland keeled over to port and lay on her port side, capsized and sank in a position some three miles off Arnanes light.

Ron: You're there and you knows there's men going down and there's nothing you can do. And when you know the men, when you've been for a drink with them, and you can picture them going down...

Maureen: He was second engineer and I'm sure he'd be in the engine room. And when I close me eyes, I can see him with the water rising up.

Stan: It was sorrow. And pity. Knowing what they were going through. Knowing what they'd gone through. And fear. I don't mind admitting it. I was terrified at the time.

Ted: We are laying over. Help me.

Maureen: He didn't want to go. He said before he went, I'll just do the one trip.

Ted: We're laying over. Give my love and the crew's love to the wives and families.

The organ finishes. Pause. Jim sings 'Harry Eddom' solo unaccompanied.

HARRY EDDOM

High on the storm torn coast of Iceland
February sixty eight
Ross Cleveland out of Hull lay hiding
With anxious eyes her skipper waits.

Gale force twelve and the black ice building
Blinding snow and the radar gone
On the cruel rocks of Isafiord
She'll be thrown before the dawn.

Try to run for the eastern seaboard
Turn her head into the gale
Harry Eddom leaves the wheelhouse
Steps into that howling hell.

Down to a grave in the icy waters
Down to a grave in the cruel sea
Over goes the good Ross Cleveland
Ten seconds to eternity.

Out in a raft on the boiling water
Bitter wind cuts like a knife
Two men freeze and die beside him
As Harry Eddom clings to life.

In the misty light of an Iceland morning
Over the rocks in the drifting rain
Shepherds bring poor Harry Eddom
Back from the dead to sail again.

The bridge lights fade to black.

SCENE FIVE

The lights snap back up.

Stan: The writing was on the wall back in the sixties. And I suppose it all started with the Cod Wars.

They break to various positions. The next section is done deliberately theatrically.

Ron: *(As M.C.)* Ladies and gentlemen, may we present for you the Decline and Decade of Destruction of the British Trawling Industry. A tragi-comic melodramatic farce in three acts. Act One, the First Cod War, 1958. *(Rings ship's bell.)*

Maureen: *(As an over-the-top Icelander.)* Ve vill vin the battle in ze end and get evveyzing that Iceland vants.

Jim: *(As upper class English politician.)* Oh dear. This is one of the most complicated international tangles it has ever been my misfortune to have to deal with.

Ron: 1961. Britain accepts Icelandic 12-mile limit. *(Rings bell. Others protest except Maureen.)* Act Two, the Second Cod War, 1971. *(Rings bell.)*

Stan: *(Jumps on table and sings in a grand operatic style.)* Down with your trawling tackle, down with your nets and gear, wait for the winches winding, wait for the deckies' cheer.

Maureen as villainous Icelander creeps up behind Stan holding a 'snapper.'

Ron/Ted/Jim: Look out, he's behind you.

Maureen pokes 'snapper' between Stan's legs and 'cuts' off his vital parts.

Stan: He's cut me frigging warps.

Ron: 1973 — Britain accepts Icelandic 50-mile limit. *(Rings bell. Protests again.)* Act Three, the Third Cod War — 1975. *(Rings bell.)*

74

Maureen: *(As shy young girl.)*
Our fishermen husbands are very brave
Dodging gunboats and big waves
We are their wives sick with worry
So send in the Navy *(in own voice.)* and bloody 'urry.

Ted: *(very pukka.)* On the first collision I damaged his port bridge wing with my anchor. On the second collision he damaged me up forrard and on the third collision he damaged me and I dented him on the starboard side. The fourth collision did most of the damage when the Baldur's stern ripped through the side of my ship forrard on the port side. Like a damned tin opener.

Jim: *(As jolly nice sailor.)* I was in the ward room at the time. I saw the fireplace lift and come towards me. The ward room bar was completely demolished.

Ted: We managed to save the photograph of Her Majesty the Queen, but I'm afraid Prince Philip was lorst in action.

Ron: 1976 — Britain accepts Icelandic 200-mile limit. *(Rings bell.)*

All: *(Protesting.)* Two hundred miles?

Maureen: Iceland three, England nil.

Stan: And that was how it ended. In tragedy and farce.

Jim: We lost the Iceland grounds, the White Sea, the Barents Sea, the Faroes and Norway. We even lost our own fishing grounds to the EEC.

Ron: It's cheaper to eat imported fish than to employ our own men in our own trawlers. And that's the nasty part of it, Icelanders catching fish on grounds we'd pioneered and landing it in our own ports.

Ted: I don't go against the Icelandic fishermen. It's their livelihood as well. But it should have been negotiated better. It shouldn't have just been thrown away.

Stan: And what people don't understand is the years of experience totalled up to what men know about the deep sea fishing. You're talking a thousand years experience just thrown down the drain.

Maureen: It's broken up a lot of families. A lot of my friends have got divorced because of the collapse of the fishing industry. It's caused friction and divorce and that's what's happened.

Ron: You'll end up with nothing but small boats in this country. And if that's what the government wants, well that's what they'll end up with.

Jim: There's nothing here at all now. There's no ships. Even the ships laid up for scrapping have gone. It's all shore-based firms, car body repairers and the like, whereas at one time it was all to do with trawlers and men.

Ted: I used to go down every day but it got that depressing I knocked off going.

Maureen: And 'Essle Road's the same. It was once a thriving community, and it's just gone. They'll never get it back to what it was. They'll never get it back to good old 'Essle Road.

Jim: And all the men that were killed and injured and drowned. And the ones that did survive, they've ended up with nothing. Just thrown on the scrap heap. If you take a walk down Hessle now you see some of the men you knew were hard working men. And you think to yourself, poor buggers. All that hard work that you've done and where are you now? You're on Social Security. Nobody wants to know you. An old sailor.

Ron: The gaffers. They wanted everything and they gave you nothing. They didn't even give us our redundancy. They didn't want to know you. If you went down there now and said to one of 'em, 'Give us a cig,' 'e'd say, 'Who are you talking to?'

Jim: You were theirs. You were their serfs. You were their deckhands.

They break. Stan comes centre stage. Music to 'Fiddlers Green' starts very quiet over:

Stan: I went down the dock, just that once. I thought, I'll just go and 'ave a look. And I stood agin the Bullnose and I thought of all the 'undreds of ships that 'ad passed in and out, all the 'undreds of men shouting 'So long Charlie,' 'So long George.' And you watched them sail away into the distance. And a lot of them men never came back. A lot were washed overboard. A lot were injured. And if you go down the dock late at night, you can see these people. You can feel 'em. You can feel them there on the dock even though it's bare. The ghosts. The ghosts of them. They was great men. There's nothing left now. Nothing left for any of us that liked our way of life. It was 'ard. It was wonderful though. Some of it.

FIDDLER'S GREEN

All:
As I roved by the dockside one evening so rare
To view the still waters and take the salt air
I heard an old fisherman singing this song
Oh take me away boys, me time is not long.

Chorus:
Dress me up in me oilskins and jumper
No more on the docks I'll be seen
Just tell me old shipmates I'm taking a trip mates
And I'll see you some day in Fiddler's Green.

Stan:
Now Fiddler's Green is a place I've heard tell
Where fishermen go if they don't go to hell
Where the weather is fair and the dolphins do play
And the cold coast of Greenland is far far away.

Chorus

Jim:
The sky's always clear and there's never a gale
And the fish jump on board with a flip of their tail
You can lie at your leisure, there's no work to do
And the skipper's below making tea for the crew.

Chorus

Ron:
And when you're in dock and the long trip is through
There's pubs and there's clubs and there's lassies there too
The girls are all pretty and the beer is all free
And there's bottles of rum growing on every tree.

Chorus

All:
I don't want a harp nor a halo not me
Just give me a breeze and a good rolling sea
And I'll play me old squeeze box as we sail along
With a wind in the rigging to sing me this song.

Chorus.

END